CW00403488

Encountering the man who saved his people

ROGER ELLSWORTH

SERIES EDITOR: SIMON J ROBINSON

DayOne

© Day One Publications 2011

First printed 2011

978–1–84625–293–8

British Library Cataloguing in Publication Data available

Published by Day One Publications

Ryelands Road, Leominster, HR6 8NZ

Telephone 01568 613 740   FAX 01568 611 473

email—sales@dayone.co.uk

web site—www.dayone.co.uk

Cover design by Kathryn Chedgzoy

Printed by Thomson Litho, East Kilbride

The life of Joseph towers above the landscape of patriarchal history, pointing us to the ultimate Saviour—as Roger Ellsworth makes so perfectly clear. Read these warm-hearted and practical pages and be edified. Ideal for both group and personal study.

R. Kent Hughes, Senior Pastor Emeritus of College Church, Wheaton, IL, USA

If you're looking for one of those disastrous studies that explore a biblical character as a model for coping with your problems, you will find Roger Ellsworth's Face2Face with Joseph disappointing; but if you're eager to see how a biblical life finds its niche in God's plan, how human crud is bundled up in God's providence, or how a suffering servant points you to an unguessable Saviour—well, then, here is your ticket.

Dale Ralph Davis, former Professor of Old Testament, Reformed Theological Seminary, Jackson, MS, and former Pastor, Woodland Presbyterian Church, Hattiesburg, MS, USA

Dedicated to the loyal members of
The Pastor's Bible Study Class
of Parkview Baptist Church,
Jackson, TN.

Acknowledgements

It is always a joy to me to work with Simon Robinson, Jim Holmes and Suzanne Mitchell in the Face2Face series. I am very grateful for their encouragement and help.

I also appreciate very much the assistance of my wife, Sylvia, in producing this book.

I should mention that my book *Faithful under Fire* (Evangelical Press, 1996) also deals with the life of Joseph, and *Be Patient! God Hasn't Finished with Me Yet!* (Evangelical Press, 2003) deals with the life of Jacob. Yet another of my titles, *Christmas Pictures* (Bryntirion Press, 2010), includes some material about Joseph and Benjamin. The reader should not be surprised, therefore, to find similar wording at a few points in this book.

Contents

Introduction

As its name indicates, Genesis is the book of beginnings. It records for us the beginning of the human race, and, sadly, the beginning of sin in the human race. It also reveals the beginning of God's redemptive dealings with sinful men and women.

God first announced his plan of redemption in the Garden of Eden after Adam and Eve sinned against him. That plan came in the form of a person, and that person was none other than the Lord Jesus Christ. He, the Seed of the Woman promised in Genesis 3:15, would crush Satan by breaking his hold on sinners. How would Jesus break Satan's hold? By receiving the penalty for their sins! This he did by dying on the cross.

To carry out the work of redeeming sinners, Jesus had to come to this earth in our humanity. That means, among other things, that he had to be born into a nation. So the book of Genesis also tells us about the beginnings of the nation into which Jesus would be born—that is, the nation of Israel.

That nation was started when God called Abram out of idolatry and promised to make of him 'a great nation' (Gen. 12:2). Abram, who was later named Abraham, fathered Isaac, who fathered Jacob, who fathered Joseph.

While that may seem to be a rather roundabout way to get to Joseph, it is important. The popular way to deal with Bible characters these days is to essentially say, 'Here is this man who lived a long time ago, and he had all these problems. But he successfully dealt with those problems, and he is in the pages of the Bible to teach us how to deal with our problems. And we can successfully solve them if we will only implement the practical lessons that this man is here to teach.'

The problem with that approach is that it divorces the Bible character from the very context in which the Bible places him or her, namely, the context of redemption. We cannot accurately interpret any of the major characters of the Bible apart from that deliberate and definite context.

So we take up the life of Joseph with that context in mind. Christianity has been turned on its head these days. Its primary focus is on God advancing our individual plans, instead of him advancing his own plan. It is God serving us instead of us serving him. It is all about coping with life in this world instead of preparing ourselves for life in the next world. The piercing question that so few seem to be willing to ask is this: If Christianity is turned on its head, is it still Christianity?

We are so impressed these days with our busyness and with the challenges and aggravations of life that we have the tendency to recreate the characters of the Bible in our own image. We read our circumstances back into the Bible. Suddenly, Joseph becomes Mr Modern-Day Busy Saint trying to make sense of it all and trying to handle it all. He struggles with a dysfunctional family, with sexual harassment in his place of employment, and with a friend who fails to keep a promise.

It is not wrong to find help for living from the life of Joseph. But it is wrong to treat his life as if it has no connection with the redemptive message of the Bible. In fact, it is the message of redemption through Christ that gives us strength for facing the difficulties and adversities of life.

What does the life of Joseph have to do with God's work of redemption? How was that work moved forward in and through Joseph? First, Joseph was the instrument God used to protect the covenant nation that would produce the Messiah. If the descendants of Israel had stayed in Canaan rather than moving into Egypt, it is likely that they would have been absorbed by the Canaanite nations and would have lost their national identity. That loss could not happen in Egypt because the Egyptians loathed the people of Israel (46:34).

So God tucked his people away in Egypt, where they could be shielded from Canaanite influence and could grow into that great nation into which the Messiah would be born. S. G. DeGraaf says of the Lord, 'He wanted to set Israel apart for a while in Egypt, for Israel was in danger of being overwhelmed by the ways of the Canaanites. Joseph had only been sent ahead so that God could use him to prepare Egypt for the reception of Israel.'[1]

We must go on to say that there was more to God's redemptive plan going on in the life of Joseph than the protection of the nation. In addition to giving the Israelites the promise of redemption through Christ, the Lord God took it upon himself to keep faith in that promise alive. He did so throughout the Old Testament period by giving the people several types of Christ. These types fall into three categories: institutions, events and persons.

The practice of sacrificing animals is the main example of the *institutional* types. The Passover is one of the primary examples of an *event* that typified Christ. Joseph is one of the main *personal* types of Christ.

I'm not saying that Joseph realized that he was a type of Christ, or even that his contemporaries realized it. But, as time passed, and as the story of Joseph became widely known, believing Israelites were enabled by the Spirit of God to see in him a picture of the coming Messiah and the work that the Messiah would do. This encouraged them and strengthened their faith.

Furthermore, we who live on this side of the Lord Jesus, and have the benefit of New Testament perspective, are able to look back and clearly see many parallels between Joseph and Jesus, and our own faith in the Word of God is solidified and strengthened.

There is yet another way in which we are to connect Joseph with the plan of redemption. Joseph plainly shows us that the plans of the sovereign God do not fail. The sometimes chaotic nature of Joseph's circumstances did not mean that God had toppled from his throne. Those circumstances were not contrary to the plan; they were part of it! We can surely find comfort in this. Our own times are chaotic and turbulent, but we can look at the life of Joseph and rest in knowing that God is above the turbulence. His plan is still on track. What is that plan? It is to bring all things ultimately in subjection to the Lord Jesus who came to this earth to perform redemption's work (1 Cor. 15:24–28; Phil. 2:5–11). The turbulence of our world is part of the plan!

Of course, we would like to know how the troubling circumstances of our lives and our world fit into God's plan, but we do not. When Joseph was going through difficulties, we may be sure that he didn't know how they fitted into the plan either, but he still loved God, trusted God and obeyed God. Let us be content to do the same until the day when God removes the dark glass and we see clearly (1 Cor. 13:12).

Note

1 **S. G. DeGraaf,** *Promise and Deliverance,* vol. i (Ontario: Paideia Press, 1977), p. 231.

1 Hated by his brothers

(Gen. 37:1–11)

J oseph's family was like no other. This was the family that was to become a nation, and this was the nation that was to produce the Messiah. The family of Joseph, then, was the family that God had graciously called to himself. It was the family of God's promises. It was the family of faith in the coming Christ. It was to be, therefore, a family characterized by believing, loving, worshipping, obeying and serving God.

When we come to the time of Joseph, this family was not what it should have been. The family called to be different from their world had begun to look very much like it. The sad fact is that Joseph's brothers often acted more like Canaanites than Abrahamites (35:2, 22; 38:2). S. G. DeGraaf writes, 'Evidently the morals of Jacob's sons had become more and more coarse. After living near the Canaanites for so long, they adopted their ways and sought their companionship.'[1]

But Joseph was different. The faith that was barely flickering in his brothers was burning brightly in his heart. That faith caused him to be grieved by their behaviour and prompted him to report them to his father (37:2). DeGraaf notes, 'The Spirit of Christ in Joseph's heart was protesting against that mixing of the holy line with the Canaanites; in Joseph's complaints, the Spirit of the Lord was bearing witness against Jacob's sons.'[2]

Those who accuse Joseph of being a nasty telltale would do well to remember that his brothers were not just naughty children but adults, and that the well-being of the whole family was tied to the way in which they all responded to God.

Joseph's concern for his family was not well received. The passage before us draws our attention to the hatred that Joseph's elder brothers had towards him. We are told that they 'hated' him and 'could not speak peaceably to him' (v. 4). We are also told that they came to hate him 'even more' (vv. 5, 8) and that they 'envied' him (v. 11).

HATED BECAUSE HE WAS THE BELOVED

Part of the hatred of Joseph was Jacob's fault. He had married two daughters of his uncle Laban—Rachel and Leah—but he had never left any doubt that he loved Rachel more (29:30).

After being childless for some time, Rachel finally conceived, and Joseph was born. Because Jacob loved Rachel more than Leah or his two concubines (Zilpah and Bilhah), he also loved Joseph more than he did all his other sons (37:3).

Jacob evidently did very little to conceal his preference for Joseph, even going so far as to make for him 'a tunic of many colors' (v. 3). That tunic, which was so clearly an emblem of Jacob's love for Joseph, must have been to Joseph's brothers an infuriating sight.

HATED BECAUSE HE WAS CHOSEN TO REVEAL GOD'S TRUTH

But while the favouritism of Jacob certainly caused his other sons to despise Joseph, that was not the sole factor. There were also those dreams Joseph had (vv. 5–11).

In one dream, Joseph and his brothers were binding sheaves in the field, and their sheaves all bowed to his (v. 7). Taking this to mean that Joseph would reign over them, his brothers were irate (v. 8).

In another dream, the sun, the moon and eleven stars all bowed down to Joseph (v. 9). The sun represented Jacob, the moon, Rachel, and the eleven stars, his brothers. Even Jacob, who loved Joseph so much, was so taken aback by this dream that he soundly rebuked Joseph (v. 10). And, of course, Joseph's brothers were, if possible, even further enraged against him (v. 11).

We must not take Joseph's dreams to mean that he was just another teenager who was full of himself. Dreams in those days were often ways in which God revealed his truth, as Jacob himself knew very well (28:10–17). And the family of Jacob was to be governed by God's revealed truth.

People who are uncomfortable with God are going to be uncomfortable with those who are close to God. The main reason why Joseph's brothers had a problem with him is that they had a problem with God.

THE MYSTERIOUS WAYS OF GOD

None of the circumstances in Joseph's family caught God off-guard or took him by surprise. God never condones evil of any kind, and that certainly included the hatred of Joseph's brothers. But neither is God defeated by the evil of men and women. He can and does use the evil that wicked people freely choose to accomplish his purposes. He would take the hatred of Joseph's brothers to put the whole family in a place where they would be away from the evil influence of the Canaanite nations.

Do we doubt that God overrules the evil of men and women to achieve good? We only have to look at what Joseph himself later said about the sinful actions of his brothers (50:20). If we are still not convinced, we need look no further than the cross of Calvary. Jesus was put on that cross by men who hated him, but God used that hatred to provide the good of eternal salvation (Acts 2:22–24, 36–39).

A PICTURE OF THE LORD JESUS

We can rest assured that the Holy Spirit of God placed the account of Joseph in the Bible to fan the flame of faith in the hearts of God's people in every generation. How it fortifies our hearts with faith to see that the Lord Jesus was so perfectly pictured centuries before he came!

As we noted in the Introduction, the first promise of the Messiah was given by God to Adam and Eve after they fell into sin (3:15). From that time forward, the Old Testament constantly anticipates the redeeming work of the Lord Jesus. One of the ways in which it does so is through the use of types. Of all the types of Christ in the Old Testament, none is so clear and glorious as Joseph. We can find him typifying Jesus time after time.

It is not hard to see the Lord Jesus in the details of Joseph's early life. As Joseph was hated by his brothers, so Christ was hated by his own people (John 1:10–11).

Why was Jesus so hated? Like Joseph, he was the beloved of his Father (Matt. 3:17; 17:5; Mark 9:7; Luke 9:35; John 3:35;

5:20; 15:9). While there certainly was a sinfulness in the favouritism shown by Jacob towards Joseph, there was no sin in the Father's special love for his Son.

The enemies of Jesus were infuriated by his claiming to be the beloved Son of God (John 5:18; 10:30–31). They were also enraged by his claim to be God's chosen instrument to reveal God's truth (John 8:37–42, 45).

It did not occur to the brothers of Joseph that he was God's special instrument to ultimately bring salvation to them. Had they realized it, they would not have hated him. Let us resolve that we will learn from their error and not hate the Jesus who is God's instrument of eternal salvation for us. Let's remember that God is free to choose the way in which he will save sinners, and the way he has chosen is Jesus. We can do as Joseph's brothers and despise God's elect one, or we can accept God's election of Jesus and bow in submission before him.

A CHALLENGE

One of the main things we are to learn from the early life of Joseph is to be faithful to God even while those around us are unfaithful. The sad fact is that there are many in our churches like Joseph's brothers. While professing to be Christians, they do not adhere to the doctrinal core of the Christian faith, choosing rather to peacefully co-exist with modern Canaanites who have no room for God.

The crying need of this day is for Josephs. The health and well-being of the church will not come from those who have settled down with the Canaanites but from those who, like Joseph, determine that they will stand against deteriorating faith and for the truths of God's holy Word.

FOR FURTHER STUDY

1. Read John 3:19–21. What do these verses teach about the person who hates Christ?

2. Read John 15:18–25. What does Jesus teach here about the hatred the world has for God's people?

3. Read Philippians 1:12–18. How did God use the imprisonment of Paul to achieve a good purpose?

TO THINK ABOUT AND DISCUSS

1. Why do you think it was necessary for God to separate the people of Israel from the Canaanites at this time? Why was it better for the Israelites to be near the Egyptians but not near the Canaanites?

2. Try to recall a time when you were on the receiving end of evil acts. How did God bring good out of that situation?

3. How would you explain God's mysterious ways to a friend?

Notes

1 **S. G. DeGraaf,** *Promise and Deliverance,* vol. i (Ontario: Paideia Press, 1977), p. 225.

2 Ibid.

2 Away with Joseph!

(37:12–36)

This passage puts before us an ugly, revolting sight. Here the brothers of Joseph first conspire to kill him and then decide to sell him into slavery. While the course on which they settled may have been less cruel than murder, it was still cruel. George Lawson is certainly correct in saying, '… it is not easy to find a parallel in history to the cruel intentions, and to the cruel conduct, of Joseph's brethren.'[1]

What prompted these men to act as they did? We can answer in one word: hatred. We have established that the brothers of Joseph hated him because he was the beloved of their father and because he was chosen by God to reveal God's truth. But there are degrees of hatred, and this was hatred to its highest degree.

THE PLANS OF EVIL MEN

PLAN A

Joseph's brothers hated him so intensely that even the mere sight of Joseph ignited within them the desire to kill him (v. 18).

PLAN B

The plan would have been carried out had it not been for the intervention of the eldest brother, Reuben (vv. 21–22). While he shared the animosity of the others towards Joseph, he did not want to be a party to bringing grief to their father. The fact that this didn't mean anything to the others tells us how deep their hatred was. Let Jacob suffer if it meant getting rid of Joseph!

Reuben proposed that they throw Joseph into a pit and let him die there (v. 22). Of course, Reuben did not really intend that Joseph should die. He planned to go back later and get him out. How are we to explain Reuben's plan? The fact that he had already broken his father's heart (35:22) may have caused him to decide not to do so again.

Agreeing with Reuben for the moment, the others seized Joseph, stripped him of the coat they hated and cast him into the pit (vv. 23–24). The fact that they were able to sit down and eat, presumably while their brother was crying to them from the pit, tells us that theirs was no small amount of hatred.

PLAN C

The sudden appearance of a Midianite caravan on the way to sell goods in Egypt sparked yet another idea in the mind of Judah (vv. 25–26). They would sell Joseph to the Midianites! This would be perfect! They would be rid of him and make a profit at the same time (vv. 25–27)! The adoption of this plan required them to come up with a story to explain the absence of Joseph to their father. So they dipped his coat in the blood of a young goat and let their father draw the false conclusion that his beloved son had been devoured by a wild beast (vv. 31–35).

So Joseph was on his way to Egypt, Reuben's good intention

was thwarted (vv. 29–30) and Jacob's heart was broken. What a fearful price tag sin carries!

THE MISSING ELEMENT IN THE PLANS

The family of Jacob was to be a family of faith in God, but, shockingly enough, there was no room for God in the minds of Joseph's evil brothers.

No thought was given to the possibility that Joseph's dreams, which they so detested, might have come from the God they were supposed to serve. These men would not allow themselves to entertain the thought that those dreams might be God calling them back to faith; they could not hear the voice of God in those dreams, or, if they did, they could not allow themselves to heed that voice.

No thought was given to the fact that, had those dreams come from God, it was not possible for them to be defeated. George Lawson observes, 'If they had cut Joseph into a thousand pieces, the word of the Lord would have stood firm and sure.'[2]

No thought was given to the fact that the pit into which they threw Joseph was not deep enough to hide him from God.

No thought was given to the fact that the Midianite caravan could not carry Joseph far enough to get him out of the view of God.

No thought was given to the possibility that they had not seen the last of Joseph or that God might have a plan that would overcome their evil ones.

The problem was not so much that these men had taken Joseph captive and sold him into slavery but that they themselves had been taken captive by Satan and had sold themselves into the slavery of sin.

THE INDESTRUCTIBLE NATURE OF GOD'S WORD

The brothers of Joseph are examples of this mindset: If you don't like the message, get rid of the messenger!

Sitting in his candlelit tent one evening, a man broke open a fig and found a worm. He broke open another fig and found yet another worm. A third fig yielded a third worm. So the man picked up a fourth fig, and then leaned over and blew out the flame of the candle. Joseph's brothers were like that man, and we all by nature are like him (John 3:19–21).

But all our attempts to put out the light of God's Word are to no avail. It is the eternal flame. We can silence its messengers, or we can succumb to the allure of feel-good religion by going to a church where the so-called pastor doesn't preach the Bible. But we cannot finally destroy the Word.

ANOTHER PICTURE OF JESUS

The treatment Joseph received from his brothers compels us to think again of the Lord Jesus. Like Joseph, Jesus was sent by his father to his brothers who hated him. The apostle John writes of Jesus, 'He came to His own, and His own did not receive Him' (John 1:11). Jonathan Edwards observes, '... Christ is one that we naturally hate, and by our wicked lives, have sold for the vain things of the world, and by our sins have slain.'[3]

Not all rejected Jesus. Some received him. The apostle John writes, 'But as many as received Him, to them He gave the right to become children of God, to those who believe in His name:

who were born, not of blood, nor of the will of the flesh, nor of the will of man, but of God' (John 1:12–13).

Is there any hope for haters and rejecters of Christ? Yes, there is! That hope does not lie in ourselves but rather in the grace of God. Left to ourselves, we would continue to hate and reject Christ. We cannot be changed by 'the will of the flesh, nor ... the will of man', but we can be changed by the grace of God that gives spiritual birth. That spiritual birth produces a new creature who breaks with his or her hatred of Christ and receives him as Lord and Saviour.

FOR FURTHER STUDY

1. Read Proverbs 16:9. What does this verse tell us about the plans of man and the plans of God?
2. Read Romans 1:18–25. What do ungodly people do with the truth of God? Why are they inexcusable in doing this? What happens to them as a result?
3. Read James 4:13–17. What do these verses tell us about making our plans?

TO THINK ABOUT AND DISCUSS

1. What evidences do you see of people living without thought of God?
2. Think about the all-seeing eye of God and the unfailing Word of God. How should these things affect the way you live?
3. Think about God's willingness to forgive those who have hated him. How does this help you in living the Christian life?

Notes

1 **George Lawson,** *The Life of Joseph* (Edinburgh: Banner of Truth, 1988), p. 13.

2 Ibid. p. 14.

3 **Jonathan Edwards,** *The Works of Jonathan Edwards,* vol. i (Edinburgh: Banner of Truth, 1976), p. 545.

3 Tested in Egypt

(39:1–20)

We can safely assume that Joseph went into Egypt with confidence and confusion. The confidence was due to the fact that God had revealed that he would use Joseph to bring his family back to faith in God. The confusion was due to the fact that he was now in Egypt as a slave to Potiphar, the captain of Pharaoh's bodyguard. How could a slave ever hope to have the kind of future that God had revealed in Joseph's dreams? How did slavery in Egypt fit into God's plan?

Joseph must also have realized that it was not his place to figure out the way in which God would fulfil his plans. It was rather his place to live the way God wanted him to live and leave the rest to God. How often we concern ourselves with the wrong thing! It is not our place to decipher God's providence but rather to practise obedience.

In this chapter we find Joseph being sorely tested by temptation. This was all part of God's plan! If Joseph himself refused to live righteously, he could never be used by God to lead his family back to righteous living. God put Joseph through the fire so that he would be fully qualified to lead.

THE SEVERITY OF THE TEMPTATION

Joseph could have entered the service of Potiphar with a sullen and bitter disposition, but he refused to do so. He rather went about his work in such a way that he gave testimony to the Lord and won favour with Potiphar (vv. 2–4). Potiphar soon promoted Joseph to be the overseer of his house and all his possessions (vv. 4–6).

God's people should never assume that they are ever out of the reach of temptation, even when things are going exceedingly well for them. Temptation soon came Joseph's way in the form of Potiphar's wife (v. 7). This was no small temptation. It came from a beautiful woman who may very well have been in a position to help Joseph. And it came not once or twice, but repeatedly (v. 10).

JOSEPH'S SUCCESS AGAINST THE TEMPTATION

Joseph could very easily have yielded to this temptation. He could have told himself that his life had been so difficult that he was entitled to some pleasure. He could have told himself that he was far from home and no one there would ever know about his sin. He could have told himself that he would yield just once and then repent.

But Joseph rejected all such rationalizations and stood firm against every advance from Potiphar's wife. He did so on these grounds:

- She was Potiphar's wife. She was married, and marriage is to consist of one man and one woman without the intrusion of a third party (2:24).
- Sin is not a small, insignificant thing. All sin is 'against God' (39:9), and that makes it a very serious matter indeed.

We must say that Joseph delivered God's truth to Potiphar's wife. He took his stand on God's Word.

We should also note that Joseph wisely took measures to avoid temptation, making sure that he was not around the temptress any more than absolutely necessary (v. 10). It has often been observed that we cannot keep birds from flying over our heads, but we can keep them from nesting in our hair!

When an occasion finally arose when Joseph was alone with Potiphar's wife, she renewed the temptation (vv. 11–12). Joseph again responded in a wise manner. He ran (v. 12)!

The evil of this woman is seen in the fact that she used the garment she had ripped from him when he ran to falsely accuse him to her husband (vv. 12–18). Potiphar responded by having Joseph thrown into prison. The fact that he did not kill him may very well indicate that he did not entirely believe his wife's story.

So Joseph had gone from favoured son, to slave, to prisoner! How his circumstances seemed to cry out against his faith!

A REMINDER OF THE LORD JESUS

The account of Joseph's temptation should remind us of Jesus. Like Joseph, he was appointed by God to be the Saviour of his people (Matt. 1:21), and, like Joseph, he was tempted in such a way that, had he yielded, he would have been disqualified from the work he came to do. But, again like Joseph, he was victorious over the temptations (Matt. 4:1–11). Our greater Joseph won a greater victory to secure for us a greater salvation!

A PRACTICAL EXAMPLE

In standing firmly against the enticement of Potiphar's wife,

Joseph serves as an example of how believers today should respond to temptation.

- We should fortify ourselves as he did with the Word of God.
- We should frequently remind ourselves of how serious sin is.
- We should quickly and decisively say 'No!' to the temptation.
- We should stay away from situations in which we know we will face temptation.
- We should be prepared to run from sin.

When facing temptations, we would do well to remember these words:

Yield not to temptation, for yielding is sin;
Each vict'ry will help you some other to win;
Fight manfully onward, dark passions subdue,
Look ever to Jesus, he'll carry you through.

Shun evil companions, bad language disdain,
God's name hold in rev'rence, nor take it in vain;
Be thoughtful and earnest, kind-hearted and true,
Look ever to Jesus, he'll carry you through.

To him that o'ercometh God giveth a crown,
Thro' faith we shall conquer, tho' often cast down;
He who is our Saviour our strength will renew;
Look ever to Jesus, he'll carry you through.

(Horatio R. Palmer, 1868)

A CONSOLATION

Joseph was in Egypt as a representative of the Word of God. There he encountered a culture that was completely opposed to that Word, and he suffered because of that opposition. Christians still suffer because of their allegiance to the truth of God. The fact that Joseph eventually arose to prominence in Egypt pictures the ultimate triumph of God's Word over all that is opposed to it.

FOR FURTHER STUDY

1. Read 1 Corinthians 10:13. What does the apostle tell us about temptation?
2. Read 1 John 1:5–2:2. What do these verses teach about the Christian's ongoing battle against sin?
3. Read James 1:13. What does this verse tell us about temptation?

TO THINK ABOUT AND DISCUSS

1. Identify the temptation that you find most difficult to resist. What steps can you take to successfully resist it?
2. What is the significance of Jesus successfully resisting temptation?
3. Identify some of the ways in which modern cultures put pressure on believers in Christ.

4 Joseph in prison

(39:21–40:23)

Having been falsely accused by Potiphar's wife, Joseph found himself in prison. Imprisonment may very well have constituted the most serious threat to his faith. From the time when he received a special revelation from God about his future (37:5–9), Joseph had seemingly been caught in a downward spiral that had now brought him to the very bottom.

His imprisonment could have caused him to give up on God. He could have said something along these lines: 'There is no reason to continue believing in God or trying to serve him. I have both believed and served and I have nothing to show for my efforts. My life is a shambles.'

But Joseph took a far different view. Instead of regarding his imprisonment as proof that God had no plan, he insisted on seeing it as *part of* the plan. His attitude can be described in this way: 'If God wants me in prison, then I will serve him in prison.'

IMPRISONED, BUT NOT FORSAKEN

God didn't simply send Joseph to prison. He went with him: '... the LORD was with Joseph ...' (39:21). To be with Joseph, the Lord had to know where he was, and he had to care enough about him to be with him. What an amazing thing! The glorious God who made all things and is worshipped by the hosts of heaven concerns himself with an insignificant slave in Egypt! And this God is not merely *concerned* about Joseph. While Joseph is there in prison, God makes him know that his God is near!

IMPRISONED, BUT BLESSED

God was not merely present with Joseph. He was present to bless! The Lord 'showed him mercy' and 'gave him favor in the sight of the keeper of the prison' (39:21).

If Joseph had gone into the prison with a bitter and sullen attitude, the keeper of the prison would have noticed; but Joseph went with a positive and happy attitude. This keeper was so impressed with Joseph that he made him the overseer of all the prisoners. And his confidence in Joseph was such that he did not think it was necessary to 'look into anything that was under Joseph's authority' (39:23).

But we must not give Joseph credit for being Joseph. All that he was and all that he received came from the good hand of God (39:23).

IMPRISONED, BUT USED

There in the prison, Joseph met Pharaoh's chief butler and chief baker, each having sorely displeased his master.

Each of these men had a dream while in prison, and each was troubled by his dream. Joseph, noting their sadness, assured them that the God he served could provide the interpretations for the dreams (40:5–8).

The butler had seen three branches producing grapes and himself pressing the grapes into Pharaoh's cup (40:9–11).

Joseph had no difficulty discerning the meaning. In three days the man would be restored to serving Pharaoh (40:12–13).

The baker had seen himself carrying three white baskets on his head. The uppermost basket, with 'all kinds of baked goods for Pharaoh', was suddenly besieged by birds, which ate the goods (40:16–17). This man hoped for a favourable interpretation as well (40:16), but it was not to be. The three baskets again represented three days. Within that period Pharaoh would have his baker executed and the birds would eat his flesh (40:18–19).

Each of the dreams was fulfilled just as Joseph had predicted (40:20–23), but Joseph, who had asked the butler to speak a good word for him (40:14–15), remained in prison because the butler apparently forgot him (40:23).

THE LORD'S PRESENCE

We can take comfort in knowing that God is always with his people, no matter how dire and dreadful their circumstances. How can we be sure of this? We have his promise (Matt. 28:20; Heb. 13:5)! We can rest assured that God would not go to the extent of nailing his Son to the cross of Calvary to endure wrath in the stead of his people and then abandon those very people!

Our circumstances will often scream at us that God does not care about us and has forsaken us. We must learn not to consult our circumstances but rather to consult the cross of Christ.

THE CHRISTIAN DIFFERENCE

No matter what our circumstances are, we must make it our

business to love, serve and trust God. Our circumstances change, but our job description always remains the same!

Every circumstance, whether good or ill, gives us the opportunity to leave a good witness for God. In every situation, Christians should distinguish themselves. Christians should be the best employees, the best students, the best neighbours, the best athletes—not in the sense of ability, but rather in terms of attitude.

THE STRANGE PROVIDENCE

Joseph's time in prison, unnecessarily extended, it would seem, by the butler's forgetfulness, must have caused Joseph to often reflect on the strangeness of God's ways.

Each Christian knows about this. The Lord has plainly said that his thoughts are not our thoughts and his ways are not our ways. Indeed, his ways and his thoughts are much higher than ours (Isa. 55:8–9).

It is one thing to read those words or to hear them preached or taught. It is quite another thing to meet the reality of which they speak, that is, the reality of God doing things far differently than we would. It is all so simple to us. If we are at Point A and God wants us to be at Point B, he should merely move us from the one to the other. After all, the shortest distance between two points is a straight line!

But God does not concern himself with taking us the shortest distance. He is much more interested in educating us while we travel the longer distance. We find proof of this when he delivered the people of Israel from bondage in Egypt:

Then it came to pass, when Pharaoh had let the people go, that God did not lead them by way of the land of the Philistines, although that was near; for God said, 'Lest perhaps the people change their minds when they see war, and return to Egypt.' So God led the people around by way of the wilderness of the Red Sea.   (Exod. 13:17–18a)

We tend to focus on the word 'around' in that eighteenth verse. Our focus should be on the words 'God led'. While we cannot understand the 'around', we can and must trust that God is leading us. He has a purpose in that 'around'!

Through the butler's forgetfulness, Joseph was being led 'around'. Point A was life in prison, and Point B was freedom, but Joseph was not moving directly from Point A to Point B! We can see the measure of this man in that he did not focus on the 'around', but rather rested in the 'God led'.

We always want to read the book of providence now. We want God to explain to us why this circumstance came our way and why the other did not. We want God to explain why we are taking the long way instead of the short way, and we want his explanation now.

But God has another book for us to read—the Bible. In that book, he tells us to concern ourselves with trusting him, even when we do not understand his dealings with us. We are to trust that he always has the best interests of his children at heart. Our circumstances will often scream otherwise, but we must never draw conclusions about what is in the heart of God on the basis of our circumstances. We must rather look to the cross of Christ. That is where we are able to see clearly the heart of God for his people. We are called to see it and rest in it.

By the way, God will eventually read for us the book of his providence. He will finally explain all his dealings with us, and all will make perfect sense, as these well-loved lines from Charles Tindley gloriously affirm:

Trials dark on every hand, and we cannot understand
All the ways that God would lead us to that blessed promised land,
But He'll guide us with His eye, and we'll follow till we die,
And we'll understand it better by and by.   (1905)

As we wait for that day, we would do well, in these words from George Lawson, to 'not judge of God's word by His providence, but rather judge of His providence by His word'.[1]

Joseph must have been mystified that God wanted him to linger in prison. What possible good could come from the lingering? Joseph may not have understood it, but as we look at the whole of his life we have no difficulty in seeing that God used those additional two years to put into Joseph the strength and the patience that he would sorely need when he was finally thrust into a role of leadership.

Joseph could have become bitter, but he chose to trust God and to wait patiently for his plan to be fulfilled. Joseph must have understood that bitterness does not change the strange providence. It only makes it harder to bear.

FOR FURTHER STUDY

1. Read Isaiah 49:14–16. How does the Lord respond to his people's fearing that he has forsaken and forgotten them?
2. Read 2 Corinthians 5:17. Why is the Christian different from the non-Christian?
3. Name some more Bible characters who experienced a strange

providence. Can you see what benefits the strange providence worked in these characters' lives and usefulness?

TO THINK ABOUT AND DISCUSS

1. *How does the realization of God's presence help us face the difficulties of life?*
2. *In what ways can Christians distinguish themselves in their places of employment?*
3. *How can you help a fellow believer who is experiencing a strange providence?*

Note

1 **George Lawson,** *The Life of Joseph* (Edinburgh: Banner of Truth, 1988), p. 27.

5 Joseph before Pharaoh

(41:1–45)

For two long years Joseph continued in prison as the forgetful butler went about serving Pharaoh. But, as we have noticed, we do not find any indication that Joseph wavered in faith or that he became bitter towards God.

Everything changed for Joseph when Pharaoh had some dreams that his magicians and wise men could not interpret (v. 8). Pharaoh's problem jogged the butler's memory. There was a man in prison who had accurately interpreted both his dream and the dream of the late chief baker (vv. 9–13)!

Joseph's waiting was over! Pharaoh sent for him, and '… they brought him quickly out of the dungeon' (v. 14). When Joseph learned that he was to stand before Pharaoh, he must have realized that this was the point in his life when his own long-ago dreams would finally be fulfilled.

JOSEPH HEARS PHARAOH'S DREAMS

Pharaoh's first dream consisted of seven 'fine looking and fat' cows coming out of the river to feed in the meadow. Suddenly, seven 'very ugly and gaunt' cows came and devoured the seven fine cows, but the gaunt cows continued to look as if they had not eaten a thing (vv. 17–21).

In his second dream, Pharaoh saw seven 'full and good'

heads of grain come up, only to be devoured by seven 'withered, thin, and blighted' heads (vv. 22–24).

JOSEPH INTERPRETS PHARAOH'S DREAMS

Pharaoh's dreams posed no problem for Joseph because he was enabled to understand them by the God who gave them.

The two dreams were one and the same. The seven fat cows and the seven plump heads of grain represented seven years of great plenty. The gaunt cows and the blighted heads of grain represented seven years of great famine. God was graciously giving Pharaoh advance warning of what was lying ahead of him and his nation. Seven years of tremendous abundance would give way to seven years of horrific famine. The fact that there were two dreams with the same meaning indicated that 'the thing [was] established by God', who would 'shortly bring it to pass' (v. 32).

JOSEPH GIVES PHARAOH A PLAN OF ACTION

While Joseph had Pharaoh's full attention, he told him what Pharaoh should do to prepare for the approaching famine. A 'discerning and wise man' should be given authority to collect one-fifth of the produce during the years of plenty so that there would be enough food during the years of want (vv. 33–36).

Pharaoh liked the plan and he knew that he had his man. Joseph, the discerning and wise man who had interpreted the dreams, was the obvious choice to be the discerning and wise man to prepare Egypt for the years of famine.

So Pharaoh made Joseph second only to himself in authority (v. 40) and set him over 'all the land of Egypt' (v. 41). Joseph, the slave and prisoner, now wore a signet ring, garments of fine linen and a gold chain (v. 42). As he rode in the second chariot of Egypt, the cry went out, 'Bow the knee!' (v. 43).

Pharaoh also gave Joseph the name Zaphenath-Paneah ('God speaks and he lives') and the daughter of a priest to be his wife (v. 45).

It must now have been obvious to Joseph that the God who had made promises to him years before was now in the process of keeping those promises.

STANDING FOR GOD UNDER PRESSURE

When he learned that he was to appear before Pharaoh, Joseph could have coached himself along these lines: 'This is my big opportunity to impress Pharaoh, get out of prison and make my own dreams come true. I must not blow it! I must not say anything to offend Pharaoh. I must make sure he likes me. I must not say anything about God, because Pharaoh has his own gods.'

Many church leaders and church people today think that the key to success is getting people to like us. So they tone down the message of the Bible. Out of their zeal to avoid dogmatism that offends people they forget about the compromise that offends God.

Joseph did no such thing. The first words he spoke to Pharaoh mentioned God (v. 16). He included the name of God four more times when before Pharaoh (vv. 25, 28, 32). In the presence of the most powerful man on earth, Joseph did not hesitate to affirm the sovereignty and authority of God.

The Lord Jesus is, of course, the pre-eminent example of standing for God while under pressure. Even though he was intensely hated, he refused to trim the truth in order to secure the favour of the religious leaders.

GIVING GOD'S 'ANSWER OF PEACE'

Joseph was sure that God had 'an answer of peace' (v. 16) for Pharaoh, and indeed God did! That answer of peace was not that there was no problem to face. There was! It was rather that there was a way to face it.

Christians are called to give God's answer of peace to the world today. That answer of peace is not merely saying that there is no problem for men and women to face. There is a very large problem—the wrath of God! The answer of peace is that the problem can be faced through the redeeming work of Jesus Christ on the cross. The apostle Paul says of Christ, 'He Himself is our peace …' (Eph. 2:14).

Have you ever wondered how Christ's death on the cross provides peace? The Bible tells us that we are not naturally at peace with God. On the contrary, we are by nature at enmity with God (Rom. 8:7). We are alienated from him (Eph. 2:17–19).

Our sinfulness is the reason for this. Because God is perfectly holy, he cannot have fellowship with sinners until their sin is taken out of the way. There is only one way that sin can be removed. The penalty that God has pronounced on it must be paid. That penalty is nothing less than eternal separation from himself.

The good news of the Bible is that the same holy God who has pronounced that dreadful sentence on sinners has also graciously made a way for sinners to be released from that penalty. The way is his Son, the Lord Jesus Christ. Without ceasing to be God, Jesus took our humanity. In that humanity, he lived in perfect obedience to God's laws. We have broken them times without number, but Jesus never broke so much as one.

After living that life of perfect obedience, Jesus died on the cross. But that was no ordinary death that he died. He actually bore on the cross the penalty that God had pronounced on sinners. He went to hell on that cross! There, in a finite length of time, he bore an infinite measure of wrath. Because he was God in human flesh, an infinite person, he could do this.

On the cross, he cried, 'My God, My God, why have You forsaken Me?' (Matt. 27:46). The reason he cried that is because he was forsaken by God. What is the penalty for sinners? God-forsakenness! Jesus was on that cross to bear that penalty.

If Jesus bore that penalty in our stead, there is no penalty for us to bear. For God demands that the penalty for sin be paid before he can have fellowship with sinners. His holy justice will not allow him to set that penalty aside. Thank God that that same holy justice will not allow him to punish twice for the same offence. Jesus bore the penalty on the cross for all who believe in him, which means that they will never have to bear that same penalty themselves.

With sin's penalty having been paid by Jesus, it no longer comes between the believing sinner and God. So the death of Jesus deals with sin and brings peace. He is God's 'answer of peace' for all who repent of their sins and trust him.

FOR FURTHER STUDY

1. Read Daniel 2:1–49. What similarities can you find between this passage and Joseph standing before Pharaoh? What 'answer of peace' did Daniel give to Nebuchadnezzar (v. 44)?

2. Read John 18:15–18, 24–27. Who in these verses had the opportunity to stand firm for Christ? How did he respond?

3. Read Acts 25:23–26:32. Who were the two powerful men before whom Paul stood? What was Paul's 'answer of peace'? How did these men respond?

TO THINK ABOUT AND DISCUSS

1. What can Christians do to keep themselves from becoming bitter towards God?

2. Identify some circumstances in which Christians find it difficult to take a firm stand for God.

3. What can you do to prepare yourself to stand firm in such situations?

6 Joseph being blessed and bringing blessing

(41:46–57)

These verses bring us to a new experience and a new challenge for Joseph. He is now powerful and prosperous. We can see how he responded to this challenge.

JOSEPH BEING BLESSED

One of the most admirable things about Joseph, and the thing that makes him such a worthy example to follow, is that he always gave priority to God. Even though he was now second only to Pharaoh, he was still living this way. When his first son was born, Joseph named him Manasseh, or 'Forgetfulness'. Joseph explained that name in these words: 'For God has made me forget all my toil and all my father's house' (v. 51).

When the second son was born, Joseph named him Ephraim, or 'Fruitfulness', giving this explanation: 'For God has caused me to be fruitful in the land of my affliction' (v. 52).

It was always God with Joseph, and now, in prosperity, it was still God. We may be inclined to think it's a very easy matter to give priority to God when we are prosperous, but it is often harder to live for God in prosperity than in adversity.

JOSEPH BRINGING BLESSING

The years of plenty came along, just as Joseph had said, and during those years he was busy laying aside grain for the years of famine. He 'gathered very much grain, as the sand of the sea, until he stopped counting, for it was immeasurable' (v. 49).

When the famine struck, the people of Egypt, who had undoubtedly been told to make advance preparations, soon ran out of food and came to Pharaoh for relief (vv. 53–54). Pharaoh responded to their cries in these words: 'Go to Joseph; whatever he says to you, do' (v. 55).

The famine was 'over all the face of the earth', so people from other lands began coming to Joseph, who 'opened all the storehouses' of Egypt (v. 56). The Joseph who had been so blessed by God was now bringing blessing to others. That is always the proper way to respond to prosperity!

So we find Joseph functioning as a saviour. He saved people from starvation in a famine-ravaged time. In so doing, he serves as a type of another and far greater Saviour, the Lord Jesus Christ.

When we come to the New Testament, we meet another Joseph—the one who was to be joined in marriage to Mary. This Joseph received a visit from an angel, who announced that Mary was to have a special son. The angel said, 'Joseph, son of David, do not be afraid to take to you Mary your wife, for that which is conceived in her is of the Holy Spirit. And she will bring forth a Son, and you shall call His name JESUS, for He will save His people from their sins' (Matt. 1:20–21).

Jesus came to this earth to be a far greater Saviour than the first Joseph. In what ways was Jesus a superior Saviour?

SUPERIOR STOREHOUSE

While Joseph opened a temporal storehouse to meet a

temporal need, the Lord Jesus opens a spiritual storehouse to meet a spiritual need.

The people of Joseph's time were perishing physically, and his storehouse was the means by which he saved them. But there is a far worse kind of perishing than physical perishing! That is spiritual perishing. It is that condition in which we are separated from God by virtue of our sins, that condition which will ultimately issue into perishing eternally. Jesus has a storehouse full of forgiveness for our sins! He has a storehouse of salvation!

SUPERIOR AUTHORITY

While Joseph had authority to open the storehouse of Egypt, Jesus opens the storehouse of salvation on the basis of far greater authority.

The authority by which Joseph operated was Pharaoh's. The authority by which Jesus operates is God's, and it is to Jesus alone that God has granted authority to open the storehouse of salvation. No one else can do so. Jesus himself said, 'All authority has been given to Me in heaven and on earth' (Matt. 28:18; see also Acts 4:12).

SUPERIOR THINGS

While Joseph did great things to open the storehouses of Egypt, Jesus did far greater things to open the storehouse of salvation.

Joseph had to plan and to work diligently for a period of seven years to make sure that the storehouses of Egypt were full. He had to exercise constant oversight. What did it take for Jesus to open the storehouse of salvation? He had to take our humanity. He had also to live in perfect obedience to God. He had to go to the cross to receive the penalty of eternal wrath in the place of sinners. He lives today to intercede for all those who come to God through him (Heb. 7:25).

SUPERIOR TERMS

While those who came to Joseph had to purchase their grain, those who come to Jesus are given salvation.

Salvation cannot be earned or deserved. It is free. The apostle Paul said to the Christians of Ephesus, 'For by grace you have been saved through faith, and that not of yourselves; it is the gift of God, not of works, lest anyone should boast' (Eph. 2:8–9).

When needy people came to Pharaoh for help, he said, 'Go to Joseph' (v. 55). We who know Jesus as Saviour do not hesitate to say to needy sinners, 'Go to Jesus!'

FOR FURTHER STUDY

1. Read Matthew 6:33. What does this verse identify as life's supreme priority?

2. Read Ephesians 1:3–14. What blessings can we find in God's storehouse of salvation?

3. Read Ephesians 1:20–21. What does Paul tell us about the authority of Christ?

TO THINK ABOUT AND DISCUSS

1. What are some ways in which God has blessed you?

2. What are some ways in which you can be a blessing to others?

3. What does the phrase 'storehouse of salvation' suggest to you?

7 Joseph's brothers come to Egypt

(42:1–24)

The seven years of plenty came to Egypt just as Joseph had predicted, and during those years Joseph had gathered grain in great abundance (41:49). When those seven years ended, the famine predicted by Joseph arrived (41:53–54). This famine was not limited to Egypt. It was 'over all the face of the earth' (41:56). Because Joseph had managed Egypt so well during the years of plenty, there was enough grain there to help people from other lands.

Joseph must have known that his own brothers would soon show up in Egypt to purchase food. So he determined that he would personally handle the international trade that Egypt was now conducting.

JOSEPH MEETS HIS BROTHERS

The day Joseph was expecting finally arrived. Ten of his brothers showed up to buy grain. (Benjamin was absent because Jacob was not willing to risk losing his only surviving son from Rachel, v. 4.)

When Joseph went out to meet them, they, not realizing that he was the brother whom they had sold years before, 'bowed down before him with their faces to the earth' (v. 6). At that moment Joseph realized that the revelation God had given him while he was still at home (37:5–10) had been fulfilled (v. 9). We can rest assured that the Word of God will finally prove to be true although our circumstances may very well suggest exactly the opposite.

JOSEPH TESTS HIS BROTHERS

We might expect to read that Joseph revealed his identity to his brothers, reminded them of the dreams he had shared with them and pointed out that they had just now fulfilled those dreams by bowing before him. We might also expect to read that Joseph then made them his slaves or sentenced all of them to death for selling him into slavery.

But Joseph had something far different and much higher than revenge on his mind. It is true that he spoke very roughly to them and accused them of being spies (vv. 7–14). But his angry tone was not the prelude to revenge. It was only a necessary element in the test that he had planned. That test was designed to bring his brothers to repentance. Joseph would manoeuvre them into a situation in which they would either abandon a son of Rachel, as they had years before, or show true repentance by standing with that son of Rachel.

For this test to be carried out, it was necessary for them to bring Benjamin, whom they had mentioned to Joseph in defending themselves against his accusation that they were spies (v. 13).

To impress upon them how very serious he was about them bringing Benjamin to Egypt, Joseph first insisted that one of their number be sent back for Benjamin (v. 16). He then put them all in prison for three days (v. 17). After those three days, Joseph took a kinder approach that allowed all of them except one to return to Canaan, with the understanding that they would come back to Egypt with Benjamin (vv. 18–20). Simeon was the brother Joseph chose to remain imprisoned in Egypt while the others returned to Canaan (v. 24). Did the sight of Simeon being bound cause these men to remember the time when they bound Joseph?

Why did Joseph choose Simeon? It may be that Simeon took the leading role in selling Joseph into slavery, or it may be that Joseph knew him to have a particularly hard and evil heart (see 49:5–6).

Whether Joseph used harshness or kindness, his design was the same—to bring his brothers to repentance. They began to show some of that repentance while they were in his presence (not realizing that he understood what they were saying), and that initial show of repentance moved Joseph to tears (vv. 21–24).

'BE SURE YOUR SIN WILL FIND YOU OUT' (NUM. 32:23)

When Joseph's brothers made their way to Egypt they had no idea that they were travelling a path that would require them to face their old sins. Perhaps they thought they had got away with them, but no one ever gets away with sin! We will pay the penalty for our sins in this life, or in the life to come, or both (Rom. 14:12; Heb. 9:27)!

Our responsibility is to keep up to date with our sins! Instead of excusing them and explaining them away, we must repent of them, claiming for ourselves the promise God spoke to his people centuries ago: 'I will forgive their iniquity, and their sin I will remember no more' (Jer. 31:34).

How grateful we should be for these words:

If we confess our sins, He is faithful and just to forgive us our sins and to cleanse us from all unrighteousness. If we say that we have not sinned, we make Him a liar, and His word is not in us. My little children, these things I write to you, so that you may not sin. And if anyone sins, we have an Advocate with the Father, Jesus Christ the righteous. (1 John 1:9–2:1)

EVERYTHING SERVES GOD'S PLAN OF REDEMPTION

We must not so focus upon Joseph as an individual that we forget the larger picture. God was in the process of bringing his people into the land of Egypt, where they would grow into a great nation away from the evil influence of the Canaanite nations. God would eventually bring that great nation out of Egypt and establish it in the land of Canaan. Into that nation God would bring his Son, who would prove to be a blessing to all nations.

To accomplish all this, God put Joseph in Egypt and then brought famine to Egypt and to the surrounding nations. Even famines serve the gospel of God! We must learn from this not to look upon events and circumstances in terms of our own comfort, but rather to see them in terms of God advancing his plan of redemption.

FOR FURTHER STUDY

1. Read Joshua 21:45; 23:14; and Isaiah 40:6–7. What do these verses affirm about the Word of God?

2. Read Luke 15:11–24. What does this parable show us about the way to deal with our sins?

3. Read Galatians 6:7–8. What do these verses teach about our sins?

TO THINK ABOUT AND DISCUSS

1. *What do you think 'repentance' means?*

2. *Identify some ways in which God has brought you to repentance.*

3. *Think about the sentence 'Everything serves God's plan of redemption'. How does this truth help you face turbulent times?*

8 Fearing without reason

(42:25–39)

Two fears are expressed in these verses, but there was no foundation for either. The very person who caused these fears harboured nothing but kind intentions for Jacob and his sons.

THE FEAR RELATING TO THEIR MONEY

As Joseph's brothers journeyed home, and probably when they were very near home, one of them made a shocking and jarring discovery. The money he had paid for the grain was in his sack! Moses writes, '… there it was, in the mouth of his sack' (v. 27).

When he told the others, they were devastated: 'Then their hearts failed them and they were afraid, saying to one another, "What is this that God has done to us?"' (v. 38).

It's worth noting that this is the first time that we find these men mentioning the name of God! Men who had callously lived without regard to God and his commandments now had the keen awareness that they were in the hands of the very God they had so long ignored! They may very well have regarded this as God's judgement for their treatment of Joseph.

We learn later that all the men opened their sacks at the encampment and discovered their money (43:21). They evidently put the money back in the sacks and hastened home to pour out to their father the bizarre nature of their dealings with the 'lord of the land' of Egypt (v. 30) and the sad news of the imprisonment of Simeon (vv. 29–34).

To emphasize to Jacob the serious nature of the matter, they opened their sacks and acted as if they were just then discovering the money. But the fear that they and Jacob felt was real (v. 35). They had in their sacks money that rightfully belonged to the second most powerful man in the world, and that man had already expressed serious doubts about them!

THE FEAR RELATING TO BENJAMIN
As far as Jacob was concerned, the returned money was reason to fear, but the demand of the man in Egypt to see Benjamin was even more worrisome. When he first learned of this demand, Jacob was emphatic. Benjamin could not go to Egypt! Jacob was sure that the trip would deprive him of his only remaining son from Rachel. Even Reuben's guarantee to bring Benjamin safely back could not change Jacob's mind (vv. 37–38). Under no circumstances would Benjamin be allowed to go!

THE GROUNDLESS NATURE OF BOTH FEARS
The common denominator in both the fears is that there was nothing to fear! In returning their money and in demanding to see Benjamin, Joseph harboured no ill intent. To the contrary, he was working towards the good of his father and his brothers.

What was Joseph's intent in putting the money in the sacks of his brothers? Perhaps it was to soften their hearts with goodness so that they would be favourably inclined towards him when he at last revealed himself to them. We might say that it was to make them fear so that he could relieve their fear.

What was Joseph's design in demanding that Benjamin be brought to him? Was it to bring additional grief to his father? Not at all! It was to put his brothers into the same situation that they had been in years before to see if they were changed men. It was to put them in a situation in which they would again have to choose to stand with a son of Rachel or to abandon him.

GOD CAUSING US TO FEAR

The groundless fears of Joseph's father and brothers speak pointedly to us about God's dealings with us. How often he causes us to fear! He plainly tells us in his Word about the reality of our sin and how very repugnant it is to him, the holy God. He stresses again and again for us the reality of judgement to come, using the most terrifying language imaginable to drive home the awful nature of that judgement (weeping, wailing, gnashing of teeth, darkness, unquenchable fire, brimstone, lake of fire, bottomless pit, etc.).

Some try to remove the terror of such terms by dismissing them as figurative language. But this is to no avail. Let's say for a moment that all of these terms are figurative. The point that comes to mind is this: How terrible God's judgement must be if it requires such figures to convey it.

GOD RELIEVING OUR FEARS

Some misconstrue God's intent in inducing fear in human hearts. They take his fear-inducing measures to mean that God is a mean, spiteful, vengeful monster.

The truth is that God brings us to fear so that he can relieve our fears. John Newton puts it in these words:

'Twas grace that taught my heart to fear,
And grace my fears relieved;
How precious did that grace appear
The hour I first believed.   ('Amazing Grace', 1779)

In Romans 2:4, the apostle Paul writes, 'Or do you despise the riches of His goodness, forbearance, and longsuffering, not knowing that the goodness of God leads you to repentance?' God's purpose in striking fear into our sinful hearts is so that we will come to see the gravity of our sins, hate them and turn decisively away from them to him. No one who finally enters the glories of heaven will complain that God brought him or her there by revealing the horrors of hell.

FOR FURTHER STUDY

1. Read Isaiah 43:1–7. How does God comfort his people in these verses?
2. Read Luke 12:4–5. What does Jesus teach in these verses?
3. Read Hebrews 10:31. What fearful thing do we find out about here?

TO THINK ABOUT AND DISCUSS

1. What truths did God use to cause you to fear before you were converted to Christ?
2. What truths did God use to relieve those fears?
3. How do you explain the unwillingness of many pastors and church members to speak to sinners about fearful things?

9 Back to Egypt

(43:1–25)

God's grace is a many-splendoured thing. Our passage shows us a few of the many aspects of that grace. Because they were not men of faith, Joseph's brothers did not realize that they were in the hands of God and that they were being graciously led along by God. They couldn't see the invisible hand that was at work in their circumstances, but this passage enables us to see it and to magnify the grace that caused that hand to work.

FORCED BACK TO EGYPT

Jacob did not want his sons to go back to Egypt to purchase more grain because the lord of the land, Joseph, had demanded that they not come back without Benjamin. Jacob was resolved that Benjamin would not go. But the severity of the famine gave him no choice. His sons would have to make another trip to Egypt to buy food, and they would have to take Benjamin with them. It all seemed so painful! They could not possibly have guessed the wonderful things that God had in mind for them.

Jacob decided that he would send a present to the man in Egypt as well as returning the money that his sons had found in their sacks. And Jacob, who was a man of faith, prayed that God would cause that man to be merciful to them (v. 14).

SURPRISED IN EGYPT

Joseph's brothers must have undertaken their second trip to Egypt with no small amount of dread. What would befall them this time? They could never have guessed the pleasant surprises that were in store for them. They were first surprised to hear Joseph's steward invite them to his master's house (vv. 15–17). They immediately leapt to the conclusion that this was merely a plot to exact revenge on them for the money they had found in their sacks. But the invitation was sincere and without any strings attached. It was due entirely to the goodness of Joseph's heart.

Their second surprise pertained to the money that they had found in their sacks (vv. 18–23). They seized the first opportunity that came their way to speak to the steward about the money, assuring him that they had brought it back along with additional money to buy more food. They must have been immeasurably relieved to hear the steward say, 'Peace be with you, do not be afraid. Your God and the God of your father has given you treasure in your sacks; I had your money' (v. 23). They must also have been relieved to be reunited with Simeon (v. 23).

Their third surprise came when they were escorted into Joseph's house, where they were given water to drink and water in which they could wash their feet. (v. 24). Their donkeys were also given care (v. 24). When Joseph arrived, they were given ample servings of food (v. 34). It was a time of bounty and comfort, and it was all due to the graciousness of Joseph.

The necessity that forced Joseph's brothers back to Egypt and the surprising developments when they got there ought to make our minds rise to a higher level to contemplate the grace of God. We can see that grace at work in the lives of these men, and each expression of grace that came their way finds a parallel in the grace that God's children have received.

GRACE PINCHING

We must not explain the severity of the famine in Canaan in terms of a freakish occurrence in nature. This was God's famine! The brothers of Joseph must have yearned for that famine to end so that they would not have to return to Egypt, but God used that famine to drive them back there. That famine was a severe mercy! We can put it like this: God's grace pinched those men before it finally brought relief.

God's grace pinches every believer before bringing him or her relief. God's grace has to hurt us before it can help us.

How did grace pinch us? It showed us the reality and the enormity of our sin. It showed us the holiness of God and made us aware that we must stand before him at his judgement seat. Grace made us tremble and ask ourselves how it could be possible for guilty sinners to stand acceptably in the presence of God. Every thought we had of sin and of judgement to come was planted in us by the grace of God.

GRACE INVITING

The same grace that made us feel the terror of sin and judgement to come also invited us to come into the banquet hall of the gospel and freely receive all that Christ has there provided.

GRACE RELIEVING

The guilt of our sins made us reluctant to accept the invitation of the gospel. How could guilty sinners be invited to such a feast? But just as Joseph's steward spoke peace to his guilty brothers, so God's Spirit spoke to assure us that with God there is grace greater than all our sins.

GRACE PROVIDING

Having been invited to dine on the gospel, and having had our reluctance to accept the invitation overcome, we found in that gospel more than enough to meet our needs. The gospel puts before us the Lord Jesus Christ who, by his perfect life and substitutionary death, is our sufficient Saviour.

FOR FURTHER STUDY

1. Read Romans 5:15, 17, 20. What words does Paul use in these verses to describe God's saving grace?
2. Read Ephesians 1:7; 2:7; 3:8. What phrases does Paul use to convey the abounding grace of God?
3. Read Titus 3:4–7. What does God's grace provide for sinners?

TO THINK ABOUT AND DISCUSS

1. What pleasant surprises have you found in the Christian life?
2. What does the phrase 'feasting with Christ' suggest to you?
3. What is the proper way to respond to someone who suggests that salvation is partially God's doing and partially ours?

10 At home with Joseph

(43:26–34)

I n these verses we continue to see God's grace at work in Joseph's dealings with his brothers. Joseph's grace was God's grace! God could have written these men off, but through Joseph he graciously sought their repentance.

We look, then, at some additional manifestations of God's grace in Joseph. May God help us to marvel as we look!

JOSEPH'S WORDS

When Joseph's brothers returned to Jacob after their first visit to Egypt, they said, 'The man who is lord of the land spoke roughly to us' (42:30). They probably expected more of the same on their second visit to Egypt. But they were invited into Joseph's house! When Joseph arrived, he kindly inquired about their father. And when he saw Benjamin, he said, 'God be gracious to you, my son' (v. 29).

JOSEPH'S HEART

The sight of Benjamin was almost more than Joseph could bear. How he yearned to reveal himself to the brother he loved! But keenly realizing that he had not yet attained the goal of bringing the other brothers to repentance, Joseph had to restrain himself.

JOSEPH'S KNOWLEDGE

When it was time to serve the meal, Joseph, to the astonishment of his brothers, had them seated in age order, from the eldest to the youngest (v. 33). He knew them even before they knew him.

JOSEPH'S TEST

Joseph also arranged for Benjamin to have a much larger serving of food than the others—five times larger (v. 34b)! This was nothing less than Joseph testing the ten older brothers to see if they had experienced a change of heart. Years before, they had despised a son of Rachel when his father gave him a special coat. Would they now despise another son of Rachel when he was given a special portion of food? S. G. DeGraaf writes, 'There they were eating again, the twelve of them together! By now the brothers were no longer envious of Benjamin, Rachel's son, because of the privileges he enjoyed. The light was shining on Jacob's house once more!'[1]

As we have noted, it was the grace of God that was at work in the grace of Joseph. We should therefore look at Joseph's dealings with his brothers as a picture of God's gracious dealings with us. Before we were saved, we were just as alienated from God as Joseph's brothers were from him, and we did not know God any more than they knew Joseph. But God graciously worked to bring us to the knowledge of himself.

GRACE SPEAKING KINDLY

God's pattern in bringing people to salvation is to first speak roughly to them. He terrifies them by showing them his holiness, their sins and judgement to come. When they feel the horror of it all, he speaks kindly to them about the work of Christ on their behalf, about his willingness to freely forgive them of their sins and about the eternal glory that awaits all who come to Christ.

GRACE YEARNING EARNESTLY

Just as Joseph yearned for Benjamin before he finally revealed himself, so God earnestly yearns for our salvation long before we actually come to the knowledge of Christ. W. Walsham How caught the yearning nature of God's heart in these lines:

I sometimes think about the cross,
And shut my eyes, and try to see
The cruel nails and crown of thorns,
And Jesus crucified for me.

Yet even could I see him die,
I could but see a little part
Of that great love, which, like a fire,
Is always burning in his heart.

('It Is a Thing Most Wonderful', 1872)

GRACE KNOWING BEFORE BEING KNOWN

Just as Joseph knew his brothers before they knew him, so God knows us in salvation before we know him. The apostle John writes, 'We love Him because He first loved us' (1 John 4:19; see also Acts 15:18; Gal. 4:9).

Loved with everlasting love,
Led by grace that love to know,
Spirit, breathing from above,
Thou hast taught me it is so. (George Wade Robinson, 1876)

When did God first love us? Before the world began! In eternity past, God the Father, God the Son and God the Holy Spirit set their heart upon us. God chose for himself a people whom he would redeem from sin and take as his own prized possession. He designated the second Person of the Trinity, the eternal Son of God, to do all that was necessary to provide redemption for them. In grace, the Son agreed to do this. The third Person of the Trinity, the Holy Spirit of God, agreed to apply to the hearts of these people the redeeming work of Christ. He agreed to come to them in their sins, regenerate their dead minds, hearts and wills, and lovingly draw them to faith in the Lord Jesus Christ.

What a salvation! It reaches from eternity to eternity! It was born in the heart of God in eternity past, it picks up dead sinners in human history and will finally carry them into eternal glory.

Josiah Conder captured the wonder of God knowing his people before they knew him by writing these lines:

My Lord, I did not choose You,
For that could never be;
My heart would still refuse You
Had You not chosen me.
You took the sin that stained me,
You cleansed me, made me new;

Of old You have ordained me,
That I should live in You.

Unless Your grace had called me
And taught my darkened mind,
The world would have enthralled me
To Your glories I'd be blind.
My heart knows none above You;
For Your rich grace I thirst;
I know that if I love You
You must have loved me first.   (Josiah Conder, 1836)

GRACE TESTING

Just as Joseph tested his brothers by giving Benjamin the much larger portion of food, so God's saving grace tests us. Are we willing to renounce our sins? Are we willing to stop living for the things of this world and begin living for God's glory? Are we willing to take God's Word as our authority and God's people as our people? Are we willing to own God as our rightful ruler? Are we willing to give time, talents, money and energy to furthering the cause of Christ in this world?

FOR FURTHER STUDY

1. Read John 3:16 and Romans 5:8. What do these verses tell us about the heart of God?

2. Read Acts 9:15. How did God explain the salvation of Saul of Tarsus?

3. Read Romans 8:29 and 1 Peter 1:1–2. What do these verses tell us about the question of whether we first know God or he first knows us?

TO THINK ABOUT AND DISCUSS

1. What is your response to the greatness of God's love for you?
2. What is your response to the awesome fact that God knew you in salvation before you knew him?
3. How much of salvation is due to the grace of God? Is faith itself something that God graciously bestows?

Note

1 **S. G. DeGraaf,** *Promise and Deliverance*, vol. i (Ontario: Paideia Press, 1977), p. 238.

11 A cup in a sack and a cry from the heart

(44:1–34)

J oseph's brothers must have begun their journey home in high spirits. The money they had found in their sacks had been dismissed as unimportant (43:23). They had been reunited with Simeon, and he was now making the journey with them. No harm had come to Benjamin, and they had been treated kindly by the very man who had been so suspicious of them.

So they must have travelled with happy hearts and light steps. Perhaps they allowed themselves to think that they were all through with Egypt and the man who was second to Pharaoh. If so, they were in for a jolt.

THE CUP IN BENJAMIN'S SACK

When Joseph had the sacks of the men filled with grain, he instructed his steward to put his cup in the sack of his younger brother, Benjamin. Joseph then sent his steward after his brothers to enslave the man in whose sack the cup was found (v. 10). Joseph's brothers steadfastly insisted that no one had stolen the cup, but it was found in Benjamin's sack (vv. 7–12).

All this was designed by Joseph to see if his brothers would be willing to let Benjamin go into slavery in Egypt, as they had been with him, or if they would stand with their youngest brother. The fact that they 'tore their clothes' with grief (v. 13) indicates that they were truly changed men.

THE CRY FROM JUDAH'S HEART

As far as these men were concerned, the only thing they could do was go back to Joseph, admit their guilt and plead for mercy for Benjamin.

Judah, the very one who had suggested that Joseph be sold to the Midianite traders (37:26–27), now spoke to Joseph on behalf of his brother Benjamin.

It was a powerful and moving appeal. Donald Grey Barnhouse called it 'the most moving address in all the Word of God'.[1] George Lawson observes, 'Judah had never attended the schools of the rhetoricians, and yet no orator ever pronounced a more loving oration.'[2]

Judah's plea falls into seven parts:

- He pleads for Joseph to hear him (v. 18).
- He acknowledges Joseph's sovereignty over him ('you are even like Pharaoh'—v. 18).
- He reviews Joseph's past dealings with him and his brothers (vv. 19–23).
- He tells Joseph what had transpired with Jacob after their first trip to Egypt (vv. 24–29).
- He tells Joseph that the loss of Benjamin would mean the death of Jacob (vv. 30–31).
- He informs Joseph about his own role as surety for Benjamin (v. 32).
- He begs for Joseph to enslave him instead of Benjamin (vv. 33–34).

The plea of Judah was so real and unaffected that Joseph

'could not restrain himself' any longer. He had to reveal his identity to his brothers (45:1–3).

THE CUP IN OUR SACK

Many these days strenuously object to any talk about human sinfulness, but there is indisputable proof of it, no matter how much we may deny it. Joseph's brothers hotly denied having his cup, but the cup was there.

What is sin? It is simply failure to conform to the laws of God. What are the laws of God? We can find them in the Ten Commandments:

- We are not to have any other gods (Exod. 20:3). Have we placed anything else before God? Have we given anything else the love and devotion that belong to him alone? If so, we have violated this commandment.
- We are not to construct any image to represent God (Exod. 20:4–6). The first commandment forbids us to worship a false god. This commandment forbids us to worship the true God in a false way. We are only to do things in worship which we are taught in the Word of God. Are we doing this, or have we fallen into the trap of diverting 'worship services' from glorifying God to gratifying ourselves? If we have, we stand guilty of breaking this commandment!
- We are not to take God's name in vain (Exod. 20:7). Have we used God's name loosely and carelessly? If so, we stand condemned.
- We are to keep the Sabbath day holy (Exod. 20:8–11). We are to lay aside even those activities that are legitimate on other days so we can focus exclusively on worshipping

and serving the Lord. Are we guilty of hijacking God's day and using it as if it were our day? If so, this commandment condemns us.

- We are to honour our parents (Exod. 20:12). We are to obey them in our young years and respect them in our older years. Have we done these things? Have we always obeyed? Have we always spoken respectfully of them?
- We are not to murder (Exod. 20:13). Jesus made it clear that this commandment also forbids harbouring hateful anger in our hearts (Matt. 5:21–22). Can we say that we have always been free of anger and hatred?
- We are not to commit adultery (Exod. 20:14). We learn from the Lord Jesus that this commandment prohibits not only the act of adultery itself but also lusting in the heart (Matt. 5:27–28). In these days in which we are constantly bombarded with sexual images, can we say that we have never had an impure thought?
- We are not to steal (Exod. 20:15). We are not to take as our own anything that belongs to anyone else. This commandment not only prohibits burglary, pick-pocketing and shoplifting, it also forbids all deceitful dealing and unjust pricing. Let us also remember that we can steal our neighbour's reputation through slander and innuendo. We also can steal from God (Mal. 3:8–12). Who among us can say that he or she is not a thief?
- We are not to lie (Exod. 20:16). Have we always spoken the truth?
- We are not to covet (Exod. 20:17). This commandment makes it plain that God requires not only purity in our actions but also purity in our desires.

It does not matter which of the Ten Commandments we consider, the answer is the same—the cup is in the bag! We have failed to obey them. We have broken God's laws. We stand guilty and condemned before him. Just as Joseph had the goods on his brothers, so God has the goods on us. And we stand before God without any plea and without any bargaining power. We may very well wonder if there is any answer for us. The answer for Benjamin came in the form of his brother Judah, and the answer for us lies in our greater Judah.

OUR GREATER JUDAH

A surety is one who stands good for another. Joseph's cup had been found in Benjamin's sack. Benjamin was, therefore, the one who was under Joseph's sovereign indictment. He was the one who was sentenced to serve as Joseph's slave, a sentence Joseph emphatically stated in these words: 'the man in whose hand the cup was found, he shall be my slave' (v. 10).

But Judah had pledged himself to be the surety for Benjamin. As Benjamin's surety, he would become the slave of Joseph instead of Benjamin. Even though the cup had not been found in Judah's sack, he would bear the penalty for it. If the penalty were slavery, a slave he would be!

In standing good for Benjamin, Judah portrays the Lord Jesus. He is the surety for his people (Heb. 7:22). Be clear on this: there is no cup to be found in the sack of Jesus's life! He was completely without sin (1 Peter 1:19; 1 John 3:5) and was, therefore, free from the indictment of divine justice. He was free to go even as Judah was (v. 17).

But the heart of Jesus was such that he could not be content to let the sentence of God's judgement fall on those he loved while he himself walked away. The heart of a surety beat inside Jesus! He submitted himself to the sentence of divine judgement so his people could walk away from it. On the cross of Calvary, Jesus took the place of his people. He received there the wrath that was due them. He went to hell on that cross so that his people would never have to endure hell themselves. He became for us a far greater surety than Judah was for Benjamin because he endured a far greater sentence. If we would avail ourselves of the work of our greater Judah, we must stop defending ourselves against God, admit that his cup is in the sack of our lives and believe in the saving work of the Lord Jesus Christ.

When Judah stood as the surety for his younger brother, he did not know for sure that he would be allowed to receive Benjamin's sentence. He must certainly have hoped that Joseph would be merciful and lift the sentence from both him and Benjamin. It was different with Jesus. He left the glories of heaven and came to this earth with the full knowledge that he would indeed bear the sentence of his people. Knowing full well that there was no way to avoid the sentence, he moved relentlessly towards it, and, in so doing, took all his people from being slaves of sin to being children of God. So we now say with the apostle John, 'Behold what manner of love the Father has bestowed on us, that we should be called children of God!' (1 John 3:1).

FOR FURTHER STUDY

1. Read Romans 3:19–20 and Galatians 3:19–25. What do these verses identify as God's purpose in giving us his law?

2. Read Romans 8:34 and Hebrews 7:25. What do these verses tell us about the Lord Jesus Christ?

3. Read Hebrews 7:22. What word is used here for Christ?

TO THINK ABOUT AND DISCUSS

1. How do you respond to those who suggest that the Ten Commandments have no meaning for us?

2. Think about the Lord Jesus as the one who willingly took your condemnation so that you could go free. In what ways can you show more gratitude to him?

3. How would you respond to someone who asks you to define the word 'surety'?

Notes

1 Cited in **James Montgomery Boice,** *Genesis*, vol. iii (Grand Rapids, MI: Baker Books, 1999), p. 1043.

2 **George Lawson,** *The Life of Joseph* (Edinburgh: Banner of Truth, 1988), p. 244.

12 What a day!

(45:1–15)

Thiis passage relates a truly remarkable day in the life of Joseph and his brothers. Years after it occurred, these men would no doubt have identified it as the greatest day in their lives. What made this day so great?

IT WAS A DAY OF AMAZING REVELATION

After hearing Judah's impassioned appeal for Benjamin (44:18–34), Joseph could no longer conceal his identity from his brothers. He knew that they had truly changed and that the time had come for him to reveal himself to them. He did so by simply declaring, 'I am Joseph' (v. 3). These words were so stunning for his brothers that we are not surprised that Joseph had to repeat them (v. 4).

How this news must have lifted the burden of guilt these men had so long carried!

IT WAS A DAY OF INSIGHTFUL INTERPRETATION

Joseph was not content only to identify himself. He also urged his brothers to join him in believing that God had used their wicked deed to advance his own purpose. He was able to say in the same breath, '... you sold me ... God sent me' (v. 5).

In verses 5–9, Joseph mentions God four times. All Bible

students quickly agree that Joseph is one of the greatest men in the Bible. We have the explanation for that greatness in these verses. It was always God, God, God with this man! He gave God priority in every situation in which he found himself. He never let the difficulty of his circumstances make him bitter towards God or cause him to stop loving and serving God.

IT WAS A DAY OF URGENT OBLIGATION

Knowing that his father had carried a burden of grief for many years, Joseph wanted his brothers to speedily make their way home with the good news that they had learned. We should note that the word 'hurry' occurs twice in this passage (vv. 9, 13).

IT WAS A DAY OF GLORIOUS INVITATION

Joseph wanted his father to come to Egypt as quickly as possible. He wanted his brothers to speak two glorious phrases to Jacob: 'you shall be near to me' (v. 10) and 'I will provide for you' (v. 11).

IT WAS A DAY OF PROFOUND AFFECTION

Having said all that he wanted to say, Joseph 'fell on his brother Benjamin's neck and wept' (v. 14). This does not surprise us. But we also read something that may very well shock us, namely, that Joseph 'kissed all his brothers and wept over them' (v. 15).

After this display of affection, Joseph's brothers 'talked with him' (v. 15). What did they say to him? It would be interesting to know.

The remarkable day described in our passage suggests

meaningful truths for us. We can get at these truths in the form of three exclamations.

WHAT A GOD WE SERVE!

God is the same today as he was in Joseph's day. He has not changed one iota (Mal. 3:6). He is so great that he is able to take even the wicked acts of people to move his plans forward.

The supreme example of this is, of course, the cross of Christ, which was an expression, at one and the same time, of human wickedness and the sovereign will of God (Acts 2:23). As we see wickedness all around us, we should not despair. That wickedness is not great enough to defeat God or to thwart his plans.

WHAT LOVE IS THIS!

The love that Joseph expressed towards the ten brothers who had treated him in such a cruel and heartless manner is truly astonishing. It is obvious that Joseph forgave these men from his heart and never held against them what they had done to him.

We are told that the Egyptians and Pharaoh's house heard about this love (vv. 2, 16). They must have marvelled at it, and so should we. But the love of Joseph for his undeserving brothers, great as it was, does not begin to compare with the love of God for guilty sinners. This love caused the apostle John to exclaim, 'Behold what manner of love the Father has bestowed on us, that we should be called children of God!' (1 John 3:1).

May God forgive us for ever taking such love for granted!

WHAT A DAY THAT WILL BE!

We surely cannot read about the day when Joseph revealed himself to his brothers without our thoughts surging forward to that glorious day when the Lord God will fully reveal himself to his people. That will be an amazing revelation! On that day he will clear up all the mysteries. It will be a day of insightful interpretation! It will also be a day when we hasten to carry out the obligation of worship. It will be a day when we will gladly hear his invitation to enjoy what he has prepared for us (Matt. 25:34). Finally, it will be a day when we will experience the love of God as never before, and we will finally love him as we should.

FOR FURTHER STUDY

1. Read Psalm 76:10. What does God do with the wicked thing mentioned here?

2. Read 1 Corinthians 13:12. What promise does this verse make to God's people?

3. Read 2 Thessalonians 1:10. What does Paul say about 'that Day'?

TO THINK ABOUT AND DISCUSS

1. What do you think Joseph's brothers said when they talked with him?

2. How does thinking about our future help us as Christians to live today?

3. How do you explain the fact that most people seem so uninterested in eternity?

13 A message too good to be true

(45:16–27)

Jacob seems to have lived under a cloud of gloom from the moment he gazed upon the bloody garment of Joseph (37:31–34). He pledged that he would go to his grave sorrowing over Joseph (37:35), and the glimpses we have of him in chapters 42 and 43 indicate that he was steadfastly adhering to that pledge twenty years after making it. James Montgomery Boice is probably correct in concluding, 'Jacob was gloom personified.'[1]

A STUNNING REPORT

The weeks involved in his sons' second trip to Egypt to buy food have to rank as some of the most difficult of Jacob's life. He must often have wondered if he would ever see them again. When they finally returned, he probably thought he could never be happier than he was at that moment. But he soon learned that he could! His returning sons announced that Joseph was still alive and was governor of Egypt (vv. 25–27).

The cloud of gloom under which Jacob had lived so long was at the verge of breaking up and going away. All that was needed was for Jacob to believe the good news that he had just heard.

CONVINCING EVIDENCE

Jacob first refused to believe his sons (v. 26). What they had said about Joseph was simply too good to be true! But after his initial doubt, Jacob accepted the report and said, 'It is enough. Joseph my son is still alive. I will go and see him before I die' (v. 28). What caused Jacob to change his mind?

THE ONES FROM WHOM JACOB HEARD

Jacob initially rejected the message of his sons while being in an inferior position. His sons had been to Egypt. They had seen and heard things there that convinced them. But Jacob, who had not been to Egypt, was declaring that their report was unreliable. It did not take Jacob long to realize his disadvantaged position. Standing before him were his sons talking about what they had seen and heard. Jacob knew them. They had become reliable, trustworthy men. They had no reason to lie. They all said the same thing. As he pondered these things, his unbelief began to melt away and faith began to pour in.

WHAT JACOB HEARD

Verse 27 says that Jacob's sons reported to him 'all the words which Joseph had said to them'. We have at least some of those words (vv. 3–13). As we examine them, we find that they include several references to God (vv. 5, 7–9). Joseph was always talking about God, and we have no trouble at all imagining Jacob saying, 'That sounds just like Joseph!' as he heard his sons' report.

WHAT JACOB SAW

The final and decisive factor in Jacob coming to embrace the report of his sons was what we may call indisputable proofs of the truth of his sons' message. Our passage sets this out in these words: 'when he saw the carts which Joseph had sent to carry him, the spirit of Jacob their father revived' (v. 27).

The carts of Egypt spoke volumes to Jacob. His sons did not have those carts when they undertook the journey to Egypt. How did they come to have them? They were clearly carts that they had received while they were in Egypt. Those carts were visible proofs.

THE GOOD NEWS OF THE GOSPEL

This passage should be of vital interest to us. It has to do with each and every one of us, because we either are or have been in exactly the same position as Jacob when he heard the news about Joseph.

The Bible claims to have a message for each of us without exception. It is a message that in many ways seems too good to be true. This message begins by telling us that we are all by nature sinners and under the wrath of God who is holy. But it proceeds to tell us that our sins can be forgiven. It tells us that God can and will declare us guiltless, and that he will adopt us into his own family. Further, it tells us that when we die he will receive our souls into his presence and will eventually raise our bodies from the grave, and that we will live for ever with him in glory.

The most astonishing thing about all of this is that God bestows all these unspeakable benefits upon us on the basis of his Son having come into this world in the form of a man and having died on a Roman cross. It tells us that this crucified Jesus is now ruler in heaven just as Joseph was in Egypt. It further tells us that Christ's kingship will one day be universally acknowledged.

All of this, I say, constitutes a message that appears too good to be true, a message that cannot and should not be believed. And many do not hesitate to say that they would like to believe it, but they find it quite impossible to do so.

Let's take note of the things that Jacob found so convincing that he had to move from unbelief to belief. Those things he found so convincing about the message he heard can also be applied to the message we hear about the Lord Jesus Christ.

THE TESTIMONY OF EYEWITNESSES

This part of Jacob's pilgrimage from unbelief to faith speaks powerfully to all who have not received Christ. The Bible's message about the Lord Jesus is credible and trustworthy. It was penned by men who associated with him and observed him very carefully. Here is the testimony of one of those men, John:

That which was from the beginning, which we have heard, which we have seen with our eyes, which we have looked upon, and our hands have handled, concerning the Word of life ... that which we have seen and heard we declare to you, that you also may have fellowship with us; and truly our fellowship is with the Father and with His Son Jesus Christ. (1 John 1:1, 3)

When Luke began writing the Gospel that bears his name, he wanted the one to whom he wrote, Theophilus, to understand that his Gospel was based on eyewitness accounts of what Jesus said and did (Luke 1:1–3). In other words, Luke wanted Theophilus to have certainty regarding Jesus Christ (v. 4).

We cannot speak to the eyewitnesses of Jesus' mighty deeds. But we have their account in Scripture, which we do well to heed.

THE NATURE OF THE REPORT

Many can testify to something very similar to Jacob's experience. As they read what the Bible has to say about the reality and the depth of human sin, the certainty of God's judgement and the nature of the salvation God has provided, they found themselves hearing 'the ring of truth'. In other words, they found the message making sense. They found themselves saying, 'Yes, of course. How could it be any other way?'

The Bible carries this ring of truth about it. There is a sense in which it carries its own authentication with it. Its words are divine in origin and in nature, and the mere reading of them oftentimes creates the conviction that they are true.

Do you today, unbelieving friend, hear the ring of truth in Scripture? If you do, God is working in you to move you to faith. Yield to his working and receive his salvation.

THE INDISPUTABLE PROOFS

Here we are confronted with the message of the Bible, a message that often appears, as we have noted, too good to be true. Is this message backed up by any kind of evidence? Yes, it purports to be the message of eyewitnesses, but does it have any corroborating evidence? Yes, it rings true, but is there any substantiation beyond that?

There are, I suggest, some proofs that are just as powerful for us as the carts of Egypt were for Jacob. The resurrection of Jesus is one such proof. This was one of the best-substantiated events in all of history. The tomb was empty. The disciples were changed. Over five hundred people saw the risen Christ (1 Cor. 15:6).

If Christ rose from the dead, he is obviously no mere man but is in fact exactly what the Bible claims, and the Bible is corroborated.

The fulfilled prophecies of Scripture constitute another such proof. Someone has counted 325 instances of fulfilled prophecy in the Bible. Each fulfilled prophecy proves that the Bible is a divine book and that its message is true and reliable.

The archaeological discoveries are yet another of these proofs. There has never been an instance of archaeology disproving some detail in the Word of God, but there are numerous instances of it confirming such details. Each of these confirmations indicates that the Bible's message is indeed true and can be trusted. It comes to us on good authority. It carries the ring of truth. It is confirmed by indisputable evidences. Those who heed this message will not find that it is too good to be true. They will simply find that it is true, and they will bless the grace of God that enabled them to believe it.

FOR FURTHER STUDY

1. Read John 5:31–47. What evidences for his claims did Jesus give his adversaries?

2. Read Acts 26:26. What did Paul affirm about the evidence for Jesus?

3. Read 1 Corinthians 15:1–8. What evidences did Paul give for the resurrection of Jesus?

TO THINK ABOUT AND DISCUSS

1. What evidences for Christianity can you use to help family members or friends who may be sceptical?

2. How do you explain the fact that many refuse to believe even when they are given sufficient evidence for Christ?

3. How do you explain to an unbeliever the phrase 'the ring of truth' as it pertains to the Bible?

Note

1   **James Montgomery Boice,** *Genesis*, vol. iii (Grand Rapids, MI: Baker Books, 1999), p. 1095.

14 Encouragement and ecstasy

(46:1–4, 28–34)

Jacob must have been thrilled beyond measure when he learned that Joseph was still alive (45:25–28) but, as the sense of exhilaration faded, he found himself facing a sobering reality. Joseph wanted him to come and settle in Egypt (45:9–11).

This would constitute a mega-change for Jacob. He was old. Egypt was very different, and perhaps dangerous. And Canaan was both his home and the land God had promised to give his descendants. These circumstances made Joseph's proposal problematic, to say the least. There certainly was nothing wrong with a visit, but was the settling God's will?

GOD'S ENCOURAGING PROMISES

Jacob had determined that he would know the Lord's will about the matter before he left the land of Canaan. He began his journey to Egypt and paused at Beersheba, which was at the very border of the land of Canaan. Beersheba was exceedingly rich in spiritual significance. Jacob's grandfather Abraham had called on the Lord there (21:33), and his father Isaac had there received confirmation of the Lord's covenant with Abraham (26:23–25). Now, while he was engaged in worship at Beersheba, Jacob received the help he needed. There the Lord encouraged him by giving him certain promises.

A GREAT NATION

First, the Lord promised to make a great nation of Jacob's descendants while they were in Egypt (v. 3). Jacob's settling in Egypt was God's purpose. If he had stayed in Canaan, his family would probably have become absorbed in the Canaanite culture and would never have become a nation. The similarity between Canaanite culture and Jacob's family made this a distinct possibility. But there was no likelihood of this in Egypt because the Egyptians themselves loathed shepherds (v. 34).

We need only to turn to the first chapter of Exodus to see how completely God fulfilled this promise. There we encounter these words: 'But the children of Israel were fruitful and increased abundantly, multiplied and grew exceedingly mighty; and the land was filled with them' (Exod. 1:7).

So God had it all worked out in advance. Joseph was sold into slavery in Egypt so that God could in due time raise him up as ruler in Egypt and Joseph could then bring all his people there. God is sovereign. His will is never thwarted or circumvented. What appears to be a defeat for him is nothing but one more step in his relentless march to victory.

GOD'S PRESENCE

Second, the Lord promised to be present with Jacob in Egypt. He said to Jacob, 'I will go down with you to Egypt' (v. 4).

Matthew Henry writes, 'Those that go whither God sends them shall certainly have God with them, and that is enough to secure them wherever they are and to silence their fears; we may safely venture even into Egypt if God go down with us.'[1]

REMOVAL FROM EGYPT

Third, the Lord promised to bring Jacob out of Egypt (v. 4). This promise included both an individual and national aspect. The individual aspect was fulfilled when Jacob's sons brought his body back to the land of Canaan for burial (50:12–13). The national aspect was fulfilled when his descendants came out of Egypt under the leadership of Moses.

UNBROKEN FELLOWSHIP

Finally, the Lord promised that Jacob would never again be deprived of Joseph (v. 4). Jacob had been without Joseph for many years. How often his heart had ached during those years! But he would never know that ache again. Joseph would be with him all the remaining years of his life, and would be there with him when he died.

AN ECSTATIC REUNION

Verses 28–34 present us with one of the most tender and moving scenes in the Bible. Here Jacob and Joseph meet after more than twenty years of being separated. Who can comprehend the joy they felt on this occasion?

NOW I SEE!

At that indescribable moment, we may assume that understanding flooded over Jacob. What had seemed so mysterious and inexplicable to him had all become perfectly clear.

Years before, Jacob had assumed that his beloved son had been devoured by beasts (37:31–35). Imagine the thoughts that went racing through his head at that time. Why would God let such a thing happen? When Joseph's blood-stained tunic was handed to him, Jacob could only see his own tiny slice of reality. He had no way of knowing about God's larger plan, a plan by which he would put Joseph in a position of authority in Egypt so that he could settle all his family members in a place where, as noted above, they could grow into a nation.

As Jacob embraced his son, he had some insight into this plan, and he must have stood in awe of it. Had we been there to ask his assessment of the way God had dealt with him, he might very well have said, 'God has done all things well.'

HOW I WISH!

When he and Joseph met, Jacob may have thought of that time, years before, when Joseph shared with him his dream that Jacob would bow before him (37:9–11). Jacob 'kept the matter in his mind' (37:11), but he failed to hear in that dream the Word of God. He should have heard it because he himself had received the Word of God through dreams, but he did not. If Jacob had detected the Word of God in Joseph's dreams, he would not have abandoned all hope that his son was still alive. He would have said something like this to himself: 'I do not know how, but my son has to be alive in order for the Word of God to be fulfilled.'

EVERYTHING IS NEW

Jacob's reunion with Joseph meant for Jacob a new life in a new place. Old things had passed away for him. All things were now new. He would never live again in Canaan.

RESTING IN THE LORD'S CARE

In one sense, we are not at all like Jacob. He occupied a unique place in the economy of God. In another way, we are very much like him. We often find ourselves perplexed and anxious about our circumstances and quick to tremble and slow to trust. Let us take consolation from Jacob's experience. Just as the Lord knew his name and his circumstances, so he knows ours. And he feels the same tender concern for us that he felt for Jacob.

It may oftentimes seem that we are not at all important to God. Surrounded by enormous trials and difficulties, we can easily conclude that he takes no notice of us. No less an authority than the Lord Jesus Christ himself assures us that this feeling is not well founded. Our Father in heaven has such an eye for detail that he marks the sparrow's fall. And we are far more important to him than sparrows. He has the very hairs of our heads numbered, and we can be assured that he is concerned about everything that grieves and troubles us (Matt. 6:25–34). How blessed we are to have such a God!

UNDERSTANDING THE PLAN

The best of all reunions lies ahead. That is when believers in Jesus Christ will be reunited with their believing loved ones. When Jesus comes to gather us to himself and to rejoin us to our believing loved ones, all the mists of life will clear and we will be lost in 'wonder, love and praise'. It will be our united testimony on that day that God made no mistakes in his dealings with us, that he had a kind and benevolent purpose even in those circumstances that seared us with pain. We see now through a glass darkly, but then face to face (1 Cor. 13:12). And when we finally see clearly, we will say, 'God has done all things well.'

REGRETTING OUR SLOWNESS

When the people of God finally enter into heavenly glory, there will be a moment when God will wipe every tear from their eyes. Before that moment, each person will feel keen regret for not having more fully trusted the Word of God throughout his or her life. When we see the glory of our Lord, we may say to ourselves, 'O ... slow of heart to believe ...!' (Luke 24:25). If we want to feel no regret on that day, we must trust and obey the Word of God on this day and every day.

REJOICING IN OUR NEW LIFE IN A NEW PLACE

Bible students have long viewed Joseph as one of the most striking of all the types of Christ. We do well to regard him as such at this particular point. Each believer may rest assured that the Lord Jesus Christ will 'put his hand' (see Gen. 46:4) on his or her eyes. And when we open our eyes on the other side of death, it will be to see our Christ in all his glory.

What newness awaits believers when Jesus comes! Dead believers will be raised to meet him in the air. Living believers will be instantaneously changed and caught up to meet them in the air. And all this will culminate in those believers entering new lives in heaven. Those new lives will be lived in new bodies. The aches and pains of our present bodies will be for ever banished. Sickness will be no more. Death itself will have died. There will be no sad funeral processions, obituary columns or cemeteries in heaven. On that day, every saint will have a body that is fashioned after the body the Lord Jesus Christ now has (Phil. 3:20–21).

And what about this new place? What will it be like? The

apostle John was given a breathtaking preview of it by the Lord Jesus himself. John says, 'Now I saw a new heaven and a new earth, for the first heaven and the first earth had passed away' (Rev. 21:1).

The final state for the believer will not be floating around on a cloud up there somewhere. No, it will be on this earth, which will then be restored to the beauty and glory it had before sin entered. If we can find much to like in this world now, with all the havoc created by sin, we will be thrilled beyond belief by the new earth, which will be free from sin.

The good news of the Bible is that those who want to share in the delights of eternal glory can do so. There is a way to heaven. It is through the redeeming work of God's Son. The call goes out from the pages of Scripture for each of us to repent of our sins and to trust completely in Christ.

FOR FURTHER STUDY

1. Read 1 Kings 8:56. What does this verse teach about the promises of God?

2. Read 1 Thessalonians 4:13–18. What do these verses indicate about the future for Christians?

3. Read Revelation 21 and 22. What do these chapters say about the Christian's new life in a new place?

TO THINK ABOUT AND DISCUSS

1. God has made many, many promises to his people. Which of these promises are most encouraging for you?

2. As far as you are concerned, what will be the best part of heaven?

3. *What is your explanation for the slowness of Christians in spiritual things?*

Note

1 **Matthew Henry,** *Matthew Henry's Commentary*, vol. i, (New York: Fleming H. Revell, [n.d.]), p. 248.

15 Testifying to the sovereignty of God

(50:15–21)

We get the impression from Scripture that Jacob thought he did not have long to live when he learned that Joseph was still alive (45:28) and when he was introduced by Joseph to Pharaoh (47:9). Yet he lived another seventeen years! These must have been very happy years for Jacob. They were spent in Egypt near Joseph.

When Jacob died, his sons buried him in the land of Canaan. Jacob wanted to be buried in the land that God had promised to give his descendants (48:3–4, 21).

AN OLD SIN RESURRECTED

After the burial of Jacob, Joseph's brothers convinced themselves that he would finally take vengeance on them for what they had done years before (v. 15). They could not even summon the courage to meet face to face with him. Instead, they sent a message that they had supposedly been commanded by Jacob to send, a message that pleaded for Joseph to forgive (vv. 16–17).

These men knew about vengeance from observing other men, and they now assumed that Joseph was like other men.

OLD GRACE REPEATED

Joseph was deeply grieved that his brothers could think that he would withdraw the forgiveness that he had granted long ago. So when they appeared before him, he showed them the same grace he had shown before (45:1–15).

In speaking to them, Joseph both denied something and affirmed something. He denied that he was in the place of God (v. 19). It was God's place to judge people for their sins (Rom. 12:19), not his place. And it is not our place.

Then Joseph affirmed, as he had before, that God had used the evil that they had done to him to bring about a good end (v. 20).

Joseph also reassured them that he would continue to provide for them and their 'little ones' (v. 21). The account closes with these wonderful words about Joseph: 'And he comforted them and spoke kindly to them' (v. 21).

The words Joseph spoke about God bringing good out of evil are some of the most loved in Scripture. These words lead us to certain truths that are just as applicable today as they were then.

THE GREAT TRUTH OF GOD'S SOVEREIGN CONTROL

The truth that Joseph expressed to his brothers is this: God is at work in all the circumstances and details of the lives of his people to achieve the purpose that he has for them. In keeping with this truth, God is able to incorporate even the evil acts of mankind into his plan. God is so great that he will not be thwarted or defeated by the evil of men and women but will use their evil to further his plan, and all without doing evil himself!

The truth that Joseph declared to his brothers was repeated centuries later by the apostle Paul: 'And we know that all things work together for good to those who love God, to those who are the called according to His purpose' (Rom. 8:28).

There are many examples of this teaching in Scripture. One is the shipwreck that brought Paul to the island of Malta. That shipwreck was anything but a pleasant experience! And Paul was no sooner safely on land than he was bitten by a poisonous snake. Another unpleasant experience! But God used the shipwreck to bring Paul to Malta where he conducted a productive ministry, and God used the snakebite to make the people willing to listen to Paul (Acts 28:1–10).

THE GREAT MISTAKES WE MAKE WITH THE GREAT TRUTH

We will always have trouble with Genesis 50:20 and Romans 8:28 ...

- if we think that we must see what the good is that God is working towards. We must remember that for a long time Joseph did not have any idea as to what God had in mind in allowing all his hardships.
- if we think that the purpose God has in mind for us is our comfort and ease. If we assume that God is working for our comfort, we will conclude that he has failed when our circumstances make us uncomfortable. But if we understand that God is working to conform us to Christ (Rom. 8:29), we will be able to accept difficulties as an essential part of that process.

THE GREAT EXAMPLE OF THE GREAT TRUTH

The cross of Christ will always be the greatest example of God using the evil of men to bring about a good end. James Montgomery Boice writes,

Never in the entire history of the world has greater evil been done—

for this was an extreme of evil practiced against one who was not only innocent of crimes but was also actually sinless. Yet from this greatest of all evils—evils that parallel but infinitely exceed the abuse inflicted on Joseph—God brought forth the greatest possible good: the salvation of a vast company of people.[1]

OUR GREAT RESPONSIBILITY

If God is sovereignly at work in the lives of his people to achieve his glory and their good, his people must not allow themselves to become bitter about their difficulties and to complain about them. They must rather seek to trust in the Lord's purpose and to delight themselves in him.

The sovereignty of God simply means that he ordains and controls the circumstances of our lives to achieve the purposes that he has established. It means that he does what he wants to do, when he wants to do it, without having to give an explanation for why he did it.

The sufficiency of God means that he gives us the strength and grace to face the circumstances that he ordains for us.

Joseph teaches us that it is not our responsibility to discern the sovereignty of God but rather to trust the sufficiency of God. In other words, Joseph teaches us to trust the heart of God even when we cannot trace the hand of God.

FOR FURTHER STUDY

1. Read Daniel 6. What are the evils to which Daniel was subjected? What is the good that came from it?
2. Read Acts 16:16–40. What is the evil that Paul experienced here? What is the good that came from it?

3. Read Acts 27:1–28:10. What is the evil that Paul experienced here? What is the good that came from it?

TO THINK ABOUT AND DISCUSS

1. How do you define the sovereignty of God?

2. How does the truth of God's absolute sovereignty help you face the challenges and difficulties of life?

3. How do you explain the fact that so many resent the teaching of the sovereign rule of God?

Note

1 **James Montgomery Boice,** *Genesis*, vol. iii (Grand Rapids, MI: Baker Books, 1999), p. 1255.

16 The bones of Joseph

(50:22–26)

Joseph was thirty-nine when he was reconciled to his brothers. He lived another seventy-one years. The Bible passes over this period with virtually no comment. It does mention Joseph getting his family settled in the land of Goshen, his reaction to his father's blessings on his sons, his provisions for the burial of his father, and his reassuring his brothers after their father's death. But these are miniscule moments in that span.

After passing over these years, the Bible gives us one more word about this great man of God. When he came down to the hour of death, he assured the people of Israel that the Lord would eventually take them out of Egypt and restore them to the land of Canaan, and he extracted an oath from them that they would take his bones with them.

UNLIKELY PROSPECTS

Joseph had spent ninety-three of his one hundred and ten years in Egypt, but he wanted to be buried in Canaan. He wanted his bones to lie in that land where the coming Messiah would live, die and rise again.

As Joseph lay dying, his mind gravitated towards God's promise that Abraham's descendants would receive the land of Canaan as an everlasting possession (12:7; 17:8). Joseph could easily have found reason to doubt that promise. Abraham's descendants were now comfortably settled in the rich, fertile delta region of Egypt. Joseph could have been seized with dismay and said, 'My people will never leave such a comfortable life in order to go back to the land of Canaan.'

Furthermore, he probably knew about the revelation that God gave to his great-grandfather Abraham, namely, that the people of Israel would be enslaved for 400 years in a foreign land before returning to the land of Canaan (15:13–16). In giving that revelation to Abraham, God didn't give the name of that foreign land, but Israel had already been out of the land of Canaan for a period of seventy-one years, and Joseph must have realized that his people were on the front end of that experience. If so, Joseph's faith in the promise could have faltered because of the bondage facing his people. He could have said, 'Once my people become slaves in Egypt, they will never be allowed to return to Canaan.' But Joseph's faith in the promise of God to return the people of Israel to Canaan was undimmed and undiminished because it didn't depend on the circumstances being right but on the God who is greater than circumstances. That's why he said to the people of Israel, 'God will surely visit you' (50:25).

The word 'impossible' does not belong in the same sentence with the word 'God', except when it is a sentence like the one Gabriel spoke to Mary: 'For with God nothing will be impossible' (Luke 1:37).

EVENTUAL FULFILMENT

The people of Israel found this to be true. The great power of Pharaoh, coupled with their own weakness, undoubtedly caused many of them to dismally conclude that God's promise to deliver them was just a pipe dream. But they soon found that Pharaoh and all his resources were no match for God. Joseph's words came true. God did visit his people in mighty power, and they were released from Egypt. And when they left, they took the bones of Joseph with them (Exod. 13:19).

The great lesson that the bones of Joseph teach us is that the promises of God are sure, no matter how unlikely or improbable they may seem.

THE BONES OF BELIEVERS

We also live in a day that makes our faith seem improbable and implausible. The modern pharaohs of secularism scorn our faith and make our lives burdensome and rigorous. The promises of God seem distant and unreal in a world that is intoxicated with itself. What are we to do in such an age? We're to do what Joseph did. We're to trust the God who has demonstrated his power and faithfulness and has given us a reliable record of those demonstrations.

One of the points at which we are to trust him is in regard to our own bones. There is a message for our bones from the bones of Joseph. It's the same as Joseph's message to his people: 'God will surely visit you.' We are all destined to be reduced to bones, but the word 'bones' is not going to be the final word regarding us. Death is not going to have the final say. The Bible tells us that Jesus is going to break through the clouds with a shout and with a blast of the heavenly trumpet, and the bodies of dead believers will be raised to meet him in the air (1 Thes. 4:13–18).

Mine eyes shall see Him in that day,
The God that died for me,
And all my rising bones shall say,
'Lord, who is like to Thee?'[1]

When our bones rise to be clothed in new bodies, the tables will be turned. The pharaohs of government, education and the media will seem distant and unreal in the presence of the Lord of glory. And we shall laugh on that day: laugh that we could even for a moment have doubted that such a day was coming; laugh for sheer joy that we dared believe the precious Word of God; and laugh that our faith has at long last been abundantly confirmed.

THE BONES OF UNBELIEVERS

The truth that God keeps his promises ought to fill the Christian with joy, but it ought also to frighten all who don't know Christ. The promise of resurrection unto glory applies only to those who are 'in Christ' (1 Thes. 4:16). The bones of unbelievers will also rise, but only to be for ever separated from the Lord and to experience eternal destruction (2 Thes. 1:9–10). The Lord Jesus put it this way:

Most assuredly, I say to you, the hour is coming, and now is, when the dead will hear the voice of the Son of God; and those who hear will live ... Do not marvel at this; for the hour is coming in which all who are in the graves will hear His voice and come forth—those who have done good, to the resurrection of life, and those who have done evil, to the resurrection of condemnation.   (John 5:25, 28–29)

The same faithfulness of God to his promises that ensures glory for believers ensures eternal woe for unbelievers.

Another promise comes into play here. It is God's promise to forgive and cleanse all those who will come to him in true repentance and faith. If you have never received Christ as your Lord and Saviour, the terrible fate awaiting the unbeliever doesn't have to be your fate. You can turn to Christ now and receive his salvation. Jesus said, 'Most assuredly, I say to you, he who hears My word and believes in Him who sent Me has everlasting life, and shall not come into judgment, but has passed from death into life' (John 5:24).

FOR FURTHER STUDY

1. Read Mark 12:18–27. How did Jesus respond to the Sadducees' scepticism about the resurrection of the body?
2. Read 1 Corinthians 15:35–58. What does Paul teach in these verses about the resurrection of the bodies of believers? What does he say about how we should respond to this teaching?
3. Read Titus 2:11–14. What is the hope of the Christian? How should Christians be living in light of that hope?

TO THINK ABOUT AND DISCUSS

1. How do you explain the fact that so many people refuse to think seriously about death?
2. What practical steps can the believer take to live each day with a greater consciousness of the glorious future that God has prepared for him or her?
3. How can you answer someone who doubts God's faithfulness?

Note

1 Cited by **Charles Spurgeon** in *Metropolitan Tabernacle Pulpit*, vol. xvi (Pasadena, TX: Pilgrim Publications, 1983), p. 707.

Face2face series

Face2face with Samuel—
Encountering the king-maker

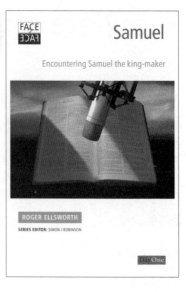

ROGER ELLSWORTH

128PP, PAPERBACK

ISBN 978–1–84625–039–2

Welcome to the world of dirt roads and oxcarts, cattle and sheep, sandals and robes! Welcome to the world of Samuel—one of the most important men in the history of the nation of Israel. Samuel was a great prophet occupying a unique position in the history of his nation. For a long time, Israel had been ruled by 'judges', but Samuel ushered them into a new era in which they were governed by kings. However, we are not taking this 'face2face' look at Samuel because we are interested in his historical uniqueness but rather because he can help us to know the God who made us and who has a wonderful purpose for all who live for him.

Roger Ellsworth has served as pastor of Immanuel Baptist Church, Benton, Illinois, for eighteen years. He is the author of twenty-seven books,

including *Opening up Philippians* and *Opening up Psalms*.

'Roger Ellsworth's book is an extremely relevant and helpful study in the life of Samuel, a much-neglected Old Testament character. It is an extremely practical, pastoral and, most important of all, Christ-exalting-character study at its best and an invaluable addition to a promising series.'

DEREK PRIME

Face2face with David volume 2—Encountering the man after God's heart

MICHAEL BENTLEY

96PP, PAPERBACK

ISBN 978–1–84625–040–8

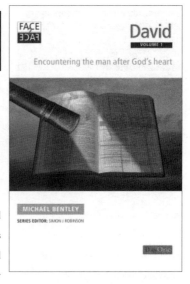

Raised in obscurity, young David would not have featured on a list of candidates for the future king of Israel-but God had different ideas! Read, here, about how God's magnificent plan unfolded in the life of this remarkable man and in the lives of those around him.

Michael Bentley worked as a bookshop manager and served in the British army before his call to the ministry. He has a diverse background, which includes broadcasting, teaching Religious Education, and holding pastorates in Surrey, South East London, and Berkshire, while being closely involved with his local community. Now retired, he lives in Bracknell with his wife, Jenny, and has five children and six grandchildren. He is the author of ten books.

Michael Bentley has an enviable knowledge of the Bible and an admirably simple way of relating its events, and then interweaving the stories with their relevance to our life. Thus, we see how the actions related in the bible can still be appropriate today in the way we live our lives.
FRAN GODFREY, BBC RADIO 2 NEWSREADER/ANNOUNCER

Face2face with David volume 2—Encountering the king who reigned in power

MICHAEL BENTLEY

144PP, PAPERBACK

ISBN 978–1–84625–015–6

Raised in obscurity, shooting to prominence in the nation of Israel, David became a powerful figure and everyone loved him—well, not quite everyone. Read about his battles, his triumphs, and also his troubles in this engaging, easy-to-use guide.

Michael Bentley worked as a bookshop manager and served in the British army before his call to the ministry. He has a diverse background, which includes broadcasting, teaching Religious Education, and holding pastorates in Surrey, South East London, and Berkshire, while being closely involved with his local community. Now retired, he lives in Bracknell with his wife, Jenny, and has five children and six grandchildren. He is the author of ten books.

'Michael Bentley treats the life of David in a simple, straightforward fashion, never losing sight throughout of the practical significance he has for us, and constantly holding before us David's greater Son, the Lord Jesus. A very good and satisfying book!'
ROGER ELLSWORTH, PASTOR OF IMMANUEL BAPTIST CHURCH, BENTON, ILLINOIS, USA, AND BIBLE COMMENTATOR

'... a book which is full of wisdom ...'
CHRIS PORTER, MINISTER, EASTHAMPSTEAD BAPTIST CHURCH, ENGLAND

Face2face with Elijah— Encountering Elijah the fiery prophet

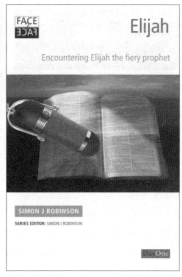

SIMON J ROBINSON

80PP, PAPERBACK

ISBN 978–1–84625–011–8

Elijah, the fiery prophet, lived in a time of intense spiritual darkness. People were openly disobeying God's commands, and true worship seemed to have been all but snuffed out. And yet God was still at work! Bringing the power of his word and Spirit into this situation, he used Elijah to break the darkness and to draw people back to himself. This fascinating encounter with Elijah draws out his significance in God's plan and provides us with practical help to live for Christ in the spiritual darkness of the twenty-first century. Each chapter includes questions and points for reflection, making this an ideal book to be used in small groups or for personal study and devotion.

Simon Robinson is the senior minister of Walton Evangelical Church, Chesterfield, England. He has also written several other books, all published by Day One, including *Jesus, the life-changer, Improving your quiet time, Opening up 1 Timothy,* and *God, the Bible and terrorism.* He also preaches and teaches in Asia and the United States. He and his wife, Hazel, have two sons and one grandson.

Face2face Sennacherib— Encountering Assyria's great and terrifying ruler

CLIVE ANDERSON

96PP, PAPERBACK

ISBN 978–1–84625–076–7

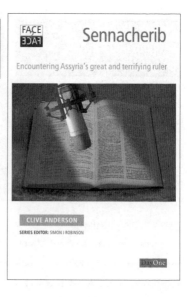

Sennacherib was once a name to send a chill down spines, yet today, relatively few have heard of him, and even fewer know much about him. Lord Byron immortalized one part of his life in a poem, but there was much more to this man than King and fearsome warrior. Coming face to face with him in this book not only reveals a complex and multi-talented man, but also the formidable enemy that the land of Judah, its king Hezekiah and prophet Isaiah were confronted with at a time of national crisis.

Today, many Christians across the world find themselves faced with situations that appear to be beyond their control. How should they react in such circumstances and what help can they expect to receive? This book, while dealing with real history, also focuses on life in the twenty-first century and gives pointers towards being faithful witnesses of Jesus Christ.

Clive Anderson is the pastor of the Butts Church in Alton, Hampshire, and a member of The British Museum Society, The British School of Archaeology in Iraq, and The Egyptian Exploration Society, and leads tours to the Middle East and Egypt and around the British Museum. He is the author of *Opening up Nahum, Opening up 2 Peter, Travel with Spurgeon, Gunpowder, Treason and Plot,* and has co-authored with Brian Edwards

Through the British Museum with the Bible, all published by Day One. Clive had spoken in the USA, Europe, and in the Far East, and is also a frequent broadcaster on local radio. He and his wife, Amanda, have one son.

'Clive Anderson brings ancient history to life. Out of the stony slabs of antiquity, Sennacherib emerges, flesh and blood. Using biblical sources and drawing on his extensive knowledge of archaeology and ancient history, Clive Anderson gives the reader a fascinating insight into the life and times of this notorious Assyrian king—enriching and sharpening our understanding of the biblical text. This book is a must for preachers and teachers and an invaluable aid to Bible study. It is easily accessible scholarship—providing accurate background knowledge, sound biblical exposition and searching application.'
REV. DR JIM WINTER, PASTOR, HORSELL EVANGELICAL CHURCH, AND AUTHOR OF SEVERAL BOOKS

'Clive Anderson brings two great passions to bear in the writing of this book. The first is that by filling in the blanks of our map of Old Testament history the key points which God highlights would be better seen and understood by God's people. The second is that from a clearer understanding of God's dealings with his people would flow a clearer desire to walk in God's ways. Both passions are plain to see throughout this book and applied with insight and wisdom by a very knowledgeable and passionate writer.'
CHRIS HUGHES, PASTOR OF BISHOPSTOKE EVANGELICAL CHURCH, HAMPSHIRE, ENGLAND

'A gem of a book'
REV. DR IAIN D CAMPBELL